LOVING YOUR CHILD TOO MUCH

How to Keep a Close Relationship with Your Child Without
Overindulging, Overprotecting, or Overcontrolling

LOVING YOUR CHILD TOO MUCH

How to Keep a Close Relationship with Your Child Without
Overindulging, Overprotecting, or Overcontrolling

Dr. Tim Clinton & Dr. Gary Sibcy

INTEGRITY®
PUBLISHERS
family
Nashville

LOVING YOUR CHILD TOO MUCH
How to Keep a Close Relationship with Your Child Without
Overindulging, Overprotecting, or Overcontrolling

Published by Integrity Publishers, a division of Integrity Media, Inc.
660 Bakers Bridge Ave., Suite 200, Franklin, TN 37067.
www.integritypublishers.com

HELPING PEOPLE WORLDWIDE EXPERIENCE *the* MANIFEST PRESENCE *of* GOD.

Unless otherwise indicated, Scripture quotations are taken from The Holy Bible,
New International Version® Copyright © 1973, 1978, 1984 by International
Bible Society. Used by permission of Zondervan. All rights reserved.

Scripture quotations marked (NLT) are taken from the *Holy Bible,* New Living
Translation, copyrighted © 1996. Used by permission of Tyndale House
Publishers, Inc., Wheaton, Illinois 60189. All rights reserved.

Cover Design: DeAnna Pierce, Bill Chiaravalle-Brand Navigation, LLC.
www.brandnavigation.com

Interior Design: Teresa Billingsley

ISBN 13: 9-781-59145-045-0

ISBN 10: 1-59145-045-4

Printed in the United States of America

06 07 08 09 LBM 9 8 7 6 5 4 3 2 1

contents

Is it possible to love your child too much?
This question is often asked and rarely answered
clearly. It's a difficult balance: loving your child
well without overindulging, overprotecting,
or overcontrolling. In these pages, we will help
parents achieve that balance as well as address other
questions such as, "How do I distinguish between
showing love and spoiling?" "How can I strengthen
my relationship with my child?" "How do I
incorporate biblical rules and limits into parenting?"
and "How can I help my child better resolve his
behavior problems?"

part one

Too Much Love . . . Is It Possible?

LOVING YOUR CHILD
TOO MUCH

chapter one

Can You Really Love Your Kids Too Much?

Every child deserves at least one person in his life
who is absolutely crazy about him.

𝒫arents love their kids. It's only natural. How moms and dads show love to their kids often differs, but that special bond between parent and child is something that has a heart of its own, something that comes directly from above. It's sacred!

Remember when you first held that tiny, wonderful being and felt your baby's warm, smooth skin? Something happened inside that locked your heart with that little one's. At the moment, you didn't believe it would be possible to love someone more, but over time your connection actually grew stronger. With the first smile, tooth, hug, steps, and words—starting with "Dada" and "Mama" and later progressing to "Can I have some money?"—your love for your child deepened.

Enter sports. You cheered wildly as he hit his first tee-ball, scored a goal, or made a basket. "That's what I'm talking about!" you screamed. "That's my boy! We're talking *big leagues* here!" You just knew he'd be good—a real chip off the old block. And if the coach pulled him out of the game? It wouldn't be pretty. No one—that's right, *no one*—better mess with your kid.

You're smiling because you know what we're talking about.

As parents and professional therapists, we love our kids with the same gusto. We know the joys, demands, and pressures of raising kids today. And we've seen just about everything—both in counseling sessions and on the court and ball field. More importantly, we've witnessed what works with kids and what doesn't.

This book is written to help you connect with your kids by identifying and explaining some of the most common pitfalls of parenting. It doesn't pull any punches or offer any gimmicks. It centers on what really matters most—building and maintaining a healthy, loving relationship with your children that is emotionally and spiritually close.

BRIDGING THE LOVE GAP

So what is healthy love? It's more than the powerful bond parents feel when their newborn is first placed in their arms, the rush of infatuation couples experience when they begin dating, or the instant bonding that can happen when friends meet. Whether with family or friends, loving relationships take work. They may begin with powerful feelings, but in order to develop true, lasting intimacy, all relationships require a commitment of time and effort—the willingness to stick with it and confront the negative feelings that will inevitably arise when we get close to another person.[1] Our kids are no exception. We can't count the number of times parents have said to us, "We love our child, but we really don't *like* him. He's so exhausting to be around."

The apostle Paul described love as hard work, writing, "Love is patient, love is kind. It does not envy, it does not boast, it is not proud. It is not rude, it is not self-seeking, it is not easily angered, it keeps no record of wrongs. Love does not delight in evil but rejoices with the truth. It always protects, always hopes, always perseveres. Love never fails" (1 Corinthians 13:4–8).

Most parents we meet strive to love their children with these biblical guidelines in mind. But what happens when their efforts fall short? The "love gap" is the distance between our good intentions as parents and what we should do to truly love our kids—and it is often what brings families to our offices seeking help. There are many reasons this separation happens, and often the disconnect occurs when parents overcontrol, overprotect, or overindulge their child.

In a speech about fatherhood, President George W. Bush noted this disconnect, saying, "It's a natural longing of the human heart to care for and cherish your child, but this longing must find concrete expression. Raising a child requires sacrifice, effort, time, and presence. And there is a wide gap between our best intentions and the reality of today's society."[2]

We can't really love our kids too much. When it comes to parenting, love—and the amount of it—isn't really the issue. Despite our good intentions, we don't always achieve healthy

LOVE COMPARISON CHART

PARENTS WHO GIVE HEALTHY LOVE	PARENTS WHO OVERPROTECT	PARENTS WHO OVERCONTROL	PARENTS WHO OVERINDULGE
See children as gifts	See children as fragile	See children as little versions of themselves	See children as possessions
Nurture kids to be unique	Nurture kids to be safe	Nurture kids to be perfect	Nurture kids to be entitled
Are respectful and supportive	Lack respect and are overly supportive	Lack respect for their child	Are overly supportive
Are kind and firm	Are kind, not firm	Are firm, not kind	Are kind, not firm
View mistakes as opportunities to learn	Allow no opportunity for mistakes	Allow no oportunity for mistakes	Believe mistakes do not matter
Practice collaborative problem solving	Believe their kids can't learn to make good decisions	Consider only the parent's will	Consider only the child's will
Believe children are a gift from God	Believe children are a fragile extension of themselves	Believe children are an investment	Believe children are an expense
Give appropriate supervision	Give too much supervision	Give directions and commands	Give no supervision
Encourage feelings and teach empathy	Avoid unpleasant feelings	Do not encourage feelings	Believe feelings are everything
Teach living skills	Teach fearfulness	Teach drivenness	Teach laziness
Get into their child's world	Censor and pry into their child's world	Force their child to enter their world	Let their child rule the world
Teach balance of grace and biblical truth	Teach that the world is dangerous	Teach a theology of works and performance	Teach pride and selfishness

love. In fact, often the problem comes with the *decisions* we make in the name of love.

The Love Comparison Chart illustrates at a glance how healthy love differs from love that tends to overprotect, over-indulge, or overcontrol. What is your parenting style?

OVERPROTECTING

Becky recently came to see us about her nine-year-old son, Michael. Every morning, Michael would wake up with a headache or stomachache, complaining that he was too sick to go to school. Becky had taken him to different doctors on several occasions, and they had run multiple tests to rule out any serious medical problems. In the end, the doctors could find nothing physically wrong.

As we discussed these problems in counseling, Becky informed us that Michael's headaches and stomach problems would disappear every day about an hour after she had decided he was unfit to go to school. They would restart in the evening just before bedtime.

"Mom," Michael would announce, "my stomach is starting to hurt again. I don't think I can go to school tomorrow."

Becky would usually tell him, "I'm sorry you feel so badly, honey. Let's see how you feel in the morning, and we'll decide what to do then."

Becky was at her wits' end. She had tried everything to help her son, meeting with school officials, seeking advice from her church pastor, and praying fervently. "I also tried sending him back to school, but that failed miserably," she told us. "Michael got even worse! He threw a huge fit, started breathing hard, and said he felt like he was dying."

"How did you feel when Michael did this?" we asked.

"Terrible . . . like such a bad mom. I felt like I was punishing him, and he hadn't done anything wrong. So I usually kept him home."

Like any good parent, Becky didn't want to see her child suffer. And Michael's tears were real—he truly did not want to be separated from his mother. Becky's desire to protect him, however, was just making matters worse. The only way Michael could heal was by going to school and coming home to find his mom waiting for him, welcoming him back. It was a difficult morning when Becky finally got her son to go to school, but it was a triumph for both of them when Michael returned safely home that afternoon.

We all want to protect our children. It's a natural, God-given instinct, an important feature of love. When we love someone, we don't want him or her to hurt! The apostle Paul stated, "Who is weak, and I do not feel weak? Who is led into sin, and I do not inwardly burn?" (2 Corinthians 11:29).

I (Tim) can relate. One afternoon at baseball practice, my talented young son Zach was fielding a ground ball when it took a bad hop and hit him square in the upper lip and nose. What a scene! Blood, busted lips, gasps, and tears. Zach was open about being afraid of getting hit again by the ball. So was his mom. But we all decided it was important to face that fear. So he went back the next week to baseball practice—the game both Zach and I love.

As parents, we should all want our children to feel safe and content. This, in itself, is a good thing. The problem comes when we overapply our love to the point that we're damaging our kids. Some children like Michael become more anxious and dependent when they are overprotected. Others rebel. One overprotective parent described his relationship with his daughter, saying:

> I see the other kids running around in the middle of the night, up to no good, making horrible decisions, and I don't want my daughter to make a mistake in her teens that she regrets for her entire life. We don't let her go out at all. Someday I think she'll appreciate that I kept her at home off the streets, away from drugs and who only knows what else. But right now it's just awful. She's depressed. I think she wants to run away from home. She yells at me, "You don't want me to have any friends! I hate you!" and slams her bedroom door in my face.

Protecting your children from the evils of the world is a God-given responsibility. But overprotecting will bruise the spirit and keep kids from growing into strong, independent adults capable of earning trust and making good decisions. Many parents tell us, "If I can only keep my child from messing up during the teenage years, he will be okay." But all kids will make mistakes—and when they do, they need to know how to learn from them and move on. The best time for them to do this is during childhood and adolescence, while there is still a safety net. If they don't learn these lessons before they're adults, they'll be left walking the tightrope with nothing to catch them when—not if—they fall.

OVERCONTROLLING

Did you know that kids are bombarded with about twelve hundred commands a day?[3] Think about what it takes just to get a child ready for school. *Zach, it's time to get up. Zach, get out of bed. Don't forget to brush your teeth. Did you wash your face? Go wash your face. Zach, come downstairs! Get the milk out of the fridge. Finish your cereal. Where's your homework? Well, go get it! Don't forget your backpack. Or your homework. Put on your shoes. Tie them. Where'd you put your coat?*

We're not saying parents shouldn't instruct their kids. Without direction, they would probably never get anywhere on time! But even the most compliant kids can keep only 80 percent of our commands. And it's the gap between 80 and 100 percent—or for some, between 60 and 100 percent—that makes both parents and kids crazy.

As one parent told us, "It seems like all I do is yell and discipline. I hate it! I feel like it's hurting my relationship with my kids." Is discipline necessary? Of course! But moms and dads must remember that corrections and commands are primarily negative interactions. It doesn't feel good to be corrected, and it doesn't feel good to be told what to do twelve hundred times a day.

No adult would want a boss who is constantly demanding and critiquing. No one, adult or child, wants to feel controlled, overwhelmed, or rejected. If your relationship with your kids consists mostly of discipline, correction, yelling, spanking, or grounding, then somewhere along the way from the delivery room to here you've lost the heart of the relationship.

Many overcontrolling parents we meet admit they often

say no before their kids even ask for permission. Kids will quickly give up on certain things like cleaning their rooms, doing their homework, and sweeping the porch, but when it comes to asking for permission, they live by the mantra, "Never give up, never give in." When parents automatically answer no to every question, they unwittingly create many unnecessary battles, ultimately making them feel even more out of control.

These parents also tend to try to manage their kids' behavior by "showing" them in detail how to respond to certain incidents. Often they monitor their children's play or conversations after observing bad or harmful behavior. Again, it's important to discipline and establish guidelines, but in moderation.

Parents who overcontrol often do so from a healthy desire to help their kids take ownership of their behavior and learn how to live within limits. The difficulty is that this method usually backfires, leading to rebellion, anger, and emotional withdrawal. When their kids respond in these ways, they tend to become even more controlling. Eventually, they find themselves being the "thought patrol," gatekeepers, or taskmasters. While we must assume these roles at certain times, our children also need us to be listeners, supporters, encouragers, collaborators, and emotion coaches.

Overcontrolling parents only want their kids to succeed. But instead of allowing their children reasonable latitude so that they might fail a few times and learn something, they train them to believe that personal success comes only through achievement—and achievement comes only through perfectionism.

Fortunately, there are other, more positive ways you can

relate to your kids that will enhance your authority as a parent and increase the effectiveness of your discipline strategies. Rather than constantly criticize, you can learn to focus on your child's good behavior, building a relationship that is based on respect as well as fun.[4]

OVERINDULGING

While overcontrolling parents tend to shut down all of their kids' requests, overindulgent moms and dads say yes to everything—toys, clothes, even privileges. We call this "Disney daddy syndrome." Attempting to shower their kids with happiness and security, these parents set no limits. One such parent explained:

> From diapers he's wanted for nothing. If he's needed anything, I've given it to him—clothes, school supplies, sports equipment. And because I grew up remembering the pain of being on welfare, his mother and I have also given him the desires of his heart—baseball cards, Lego sets, a trampoline, two puppies, a rabbit, and even a backyard swimming pool. My wife, Emma, stays home to care for Jimmy, and even though that's a full-time job, we're more concerned about lightening Jimmy's load. "What's the point of childhood if it's cluttered with chores?" we say. So Emma takes care of the animals, the laundry, and everything else at home, and I work long hours and bring home a good paycheck. You'd think we would be a happy family, but lately we feel like Jimmy has betrayed us. He's become an angry, defiant, miserable child. We just don't know what to do.

This certainly doesn't prepare kids to mature into responsible adults. As this father discovered, such spoiling only breeds discontent. Overindulged children become addicted to the cult of the next thing: as they are given each new toy or liberty, the newness wears off more and more quickly, creating a cycle of dissatisfaction and greed. Soon these parents become frustrated, angry, and resentful that their kids have become so spoiled. But they still can't say no. It's the only way they know how to give and receive love.

This spoiling also extends to household chores. Just as these kids beg and plead for the latest iPod, they put up a fight to get out of cleaning their rooms. And if their parents put their foot down, they collapse to the floor in a tantrum-induced heap. Although the children are perfectly capable of carrying out simple household tasks—taking out the trash, cleaning off the dinner table, or folding the laundry—overindulging parents won't make them help, despite the fact they are becoming increasingly angry and resentful at being virtual prisoners to their children.

The reasons parents overindulge range from guilt to issues from their own childhood. But the dangers of overindulging are real, and go much deeper than just having a "spoiled" kid. Even though kids fight it every step of the way, they need structure and responsibility in their lives. Without it they become increasingly insecure, irritable, and bored.

As our heavenly Father, God doesn't always give us everything we want, but He does provide everything we *need* (see Matthew 6). By following His example and other biblical guidelines, we can break the cycle of capitulation. It is possible to give good things to our kids in a way that, rather than overindulging them, promotes health and joy.

BRINGING UP KIDS TODAY

Parenting is an amazing opportunity! When God blesses us with children, He gives us a little one who absorbs everything we say and do. When kids are small, they smile when we smile, squeeze hands when we squeeze hands, high-five when we high-five, kiss when we kiss, and even spit when we spit. And yes, if we yell, they learn to yell. Criticize, and they learn to criticize. The influence factor is enormous.

But parenting has gotten more complicated over the years. A recent article in *The Wall Street Journal*[5] described today's kids as reading, writing, and rushing—which means moms and dads are rushing too. There's schoolwork, lunches, baths, cleaning, basketball, baseball, soccer, swimming, piano, computers, parties, doctor appointments, church programs. It seems as if all we do as parents is go, go, go. Pile on work demands, personal illnesses and losses, marital expectations and problems, money challenges, and caring for aging parents, and it seems impossible to stay relaxed enough to keep from grounding the kids for forgetting to replace the cap on the toothpaste!

Not only are parents stressed, but kids are too. We'd like to believe that our kids are immune to the anxiety, chaos, and pain of our lives, but they aren't. Children and adolescents today are facing issues that were not present a generation ago. Health education is now sex education, and children are often exposed to drug trafficking before leaving elementary school.[6] Nearly 40 percent of children fall asleep in homes where their fathers are not present.[7] And currently, for African Americans, single-parent households outnumber married-couple families.[8] Still not convinced? Consider this:

Every 9 seconds   a high school student drops out.

Every 23 seconds   an unmarried mother gives birth.

Every 4 minutes   a child is arrested for drug abuse.

Every 8 minutes   a child is arrested for violent crimes.

Every 41 minutes   a child or teen dies in an accident.

Every 5 hours   a child or teen commits suicide.

Can you believe that every five hours a child or teen commits suicide? Suicide is the sixth-leading cause of death for five- to fourteen-year-olds and the third-leading cause of death for fifteen-to twenty-four-year-olds.[9] What's even more shocking is that the second leading cause of death for Americans aged fifteen to twenty-four years is homicide![10]

Sometimes it seems as if everything in this world works against relationships and competes with our love and affection for each other. Not surprisingly, research shows that marital satisfaction goes down after the birth of a child, typically hits rock bottom during the teenage years, and never fully recovers until the child leaves home.[11] Now there may be any number of reasons for this, but we believe it underscores the fact that parenting is tough work. And most of us are not prepared for all the demands and pressures.

What's more, if you have a special needs or "extra effort" child—for instance, one who is irritable, is strong willed, has trouble focusing, or is defiant—the burden can be overwhelming. With these children, even small things can be a challenge. Their temper gauge can go from zero to one hundred in a matter of minutes. These extra-effort children need more attention, more positive interaction, more guidance than other kids, and they're great at throwing curveballs at their moms and dads.[12]

It's no wonder that with all the pressure and problems facing families, so many parents are stressed out and in need of help. Ask yourself the following questions to identify your own stress quotient:

Key Questions for Parents Under Pressure

- Do you feel like you work your heart out but aren't appreciated for it?

- Do you feel like you have to be the "heavy" with your kids, constantly correcting and disciplining them?

- Are you giving your all as a parent only to see your child's behavior and your relationship together get worse by the day?

- Do you feel guilty because, even though you love your kids, you often feel stressed or hopeless around them?

- Do you ever feel resented by your child?

If you answered yes to any of these questions, you may be coping with the pressure by overprotecting, overindulging, or overcontrolling. Every day we meet moms and dads who have gotten trapped in unhealthy methods of parenting because it's the only way they know how to love. But the good news is that the vast majority of these parents want to do the right thing for their kids. They are stepping up to the plate and giving it their all,[13] working night and day to give their kids the best of everything—from education to discipline to spiritual integrity. In fact, the results of a recent survey show that these moms and dads are more committed to parenting than those of generations past.[14] They are beginning to understand the demands of raising kids, and many are working to correct the mistakes their parents made. As one father explained to us, "When I grew up my dad wasn't there, and I'm not going to do that to my kid."

Most parents we counsel are working hard to raise their kids well, but find that the more they "love," the more distant, depressed, or defiant their kids become. If you yearn for closeness with your kids but feel that nothing is working, keep reading. This book will empower you to change! Many parents have used the principles outlined here to help their children become healthier, more obedient, and more able to control their emotions. In doing so, their relationship with their kids has grown and improved—to the point that they actually *like* being with one another again.

Every child deserves at least one person who is crazy about him or her, and we want that person to be you. Please, walk with us . . .

chapter two

How We Love Too Much

I have loved you with an everlasting love.
—Jeremiah 31:3

As counselors, we've found that a majority of the work in therapy is getting people to identify and recognize their own unhealthy behavior. But what does toxic love look like? How do we know if we're overcontrolling, overprotecting, or overindulging?

We've described common behaviors of parents who love too much. As you read, be open to what God might be trying to tell you about how you parent. One of the most difficult challenges in life is seeing ourselves for who and what we really are—but it is only when we recognize our mistakes that we can move forward.

WAYS WE OVERPROTECT

WE LIE ABOUT REAL LIFE.

We believe—and many experts agree—that you should always tell your kids the truth. Of course, that doesn't mean that you dump the harsh realities of life on them when they're too young to understand, or when it's just too frightening. But you should truthfully answer their questions in a way that's age appropriate.

For instance, if your son's beloved dog has passed away, you shouldn't tell him that you sent Muffin to live on a ranch with her sisters and brothers. However painful it is, you need to explain, "Muffin has died, sweetie, so she won't be with us anymore. But she's much better off now. She's in heaven with Jesus, and someday you'll see her again." (Do all dogs go to heaven?) Smile.

Similarly, if your four-year-old daughter wants to know where babies come from, you could explain simply, "Well, sometimes God blesses mommies and daddies with a baby to love. It was the happiest day of my life when I learned I was pregnant with a little girl."

We shouldn't tell "white lies" to our children by teaching them fantasies instead of the truth. When we tell Maddie that she'll marry a prince or tell James he'll definitely be the next hot NBA star or recording artist, we'll eventually lose credibility with our kids.

WE RESCUE THEM FROM EVERYTHING.

Rescuing is not all bad. We're supposed to look after our kids emotionally, physically, and spiritually. After all, our heavenly Father takes care of us! When He sent His Son Jesus to die on the cross, He rescued us from our sin, saving us from hell and enabling us to spend eternity with Him in heaven (John 3:16).

But some parents rescue their kids far too often, and when they do, their children don't learn responsibility. For example, Aidan won't learn anything when his mother finishes the homework he forgot to do before bedtime. Or when she saves him from suspension, telling the principal that her son wasn't cutting class, he was sick, and she forgot to call in to excuse him. That kind of rescuing isn't love. It keeps kids from learning about accountability, responsibility, and the consequences of their decisions.

WE TAKE RESPONSIBILITY FOR THINGS THEY SHOULD DO THEMSELVES.

There's a balance between letting our kids have fun and still promoting old-fashioned hard work. Parents who overprotect often encourage their kids to be lazy by doing things that the kids should do themselves. For example, they might clean their kids' rooms and put away the toys in the family room while their children are outside playing with their friends.

Even young kids are capable of taking care of things and helping with some household chores. They can pack lunches, wash cars, make the bed, dust, clean the toilets, weed the flowerbeds, load the dishwasher, even empty the garbage . . . By doing any one of these things, they can help keep the household running.

WE FIGHT THEIR BATTLES.

Some battles are best left for our kids to fight on their own. Imagine how ridiculous it would be if Ryan's thirty-four-year-old dad showed up to fight the school bully for him! Of course, most of the confrontations our kids face aren't physical, but some parents still become unnecessarily involved in minor disputes between kids and their peers.

Often, kids have been sheltered from situations where they might have benefited from problem solving or "emotion coaching" (which we discuss in chapter 12). For example, an overprotective mother may restrict her son from playing with the neighbor boy if he and the other child are having trouble getting along. As a result, the child learns to avoid difficult situations rather than to deal effectively with conflict.

WE DON'T PUSH THEM ENOUGH.

By the time he was in tenth grade, Matt had tried every instrument, played every sport, and taken every lesson possible—for about a month or so. With every new activity it was the same: he would get excited about his new challenge, but as soon as the guitar lessons proved difficult, or he wasn't scoring enough goals in soccer, he would quit and try something else.

As parents, it's our job to train our kids so they'll be strong enough to take on life's challenges. This process should be similar to the way athletes weight train. During the training process, they do a series of repetitions at one weight, and then add a little more weight and do a few more repetitions. Too little weight, and their muscles won't increase. Too much, and their muscles will tear. If we want our kids to develop emotionally and spiritually, we need to provide the right amount of pressure, encouraging them to exercise their "muscles." We must encourage, stretch, and push our children even if that means they fail once in a while.

HOW WE OVERINDULGE

WE ALWAYS GIVE IN.

When our kids ask, coo, and cry, they pull on our heartstrings. And they should! We truly believe God designed our children that way. Jesus says, "Which of you, if his son asks for bread, will give him a stone? Or if he asks for a fish, will give him a snake? If you, then . . . know how to give good gifts to your children, how much more will your Father in heaven give good gifts to those who ask him!" (Matthew 7:9–11).

As the Bible indicates, it's natural and good for us to respond promptly to their needs. The problem comes when we give in to whatever our children want—when all they have to do is whine, "But Mooom!!"

One mother told us, "It happens every time. We're standing in line at the grocery store, and Kaitlyn starts flopping around like a fish! She begins chanting, 'I want it, I want it, I want it!' getting louder and louder with each demand. It's embarrassing. I can tell people are looking at me like, 'Lady, control your child,' but when I try, she only screams more! I have no idea what to do, so I usually just cave in, throwing whatever it is she wants into the cart. I know it only makes things worse for next time. But I guess I'll cross that bridge when I get to it."

WE BRIBE THEM.

Most parents believe their children need to learn responsibility. Instead of teaching it to them, however, overindulging parents often buy their kids' cooperation. "If you empty the trash," they cajole, "I'll get you the CD." "If you clear the dinner table, I'll let you stay up an extra hour." But the bribes eventually run out, and the kids soon realize they'll get what's being offered anyway by substituting a tantrum for the duty requested. In the end, these moms and dads feel trapped and helpless to do anything but give in. Consequently, their children never really become productive members of the family, learning that being part of a team only holds you back, and limits are for those who haven't learned the fine art of throwing a fit.

WE GIVE EXCESSIVELY.

When we're buried in "things," we certainly don't appreciate what's been heaped on us. We never learn to do without or improvise. Ironically, as our rooms fill with stuff, our hearts become empty.

One rule of thumb we teach parents is that kids shouldn't get something without first making some kind of effort to obtain that item on their own. Nothing, except love, comes for free. And children should not be sheltered from this reality. Believe it or not, kids want and need the attention, love, and support of their parents far more than the newest Barbie or cell phone.

WE'RE PERMISSIVE.

Once in a while, kids need to have the freedom to venture out into the world and see how they do. But their forays into new territory need to be reasonably safe and age appropriate. Parents who are too permissive often leave their kids unsupervised for extended periods of time, or don't ask enough questions to ensure their kids will be safe from dangerous people or situations. They passively indulge their kids by not setting enough limits, hoping to make them happy. In the end, however, they're only helping their children hurt themselves.

WE GIVE UNDESERVED OR EXCESSIVE PRAISE.

Don't misunderstand us—praise is good! But praise should be earned. Praising children excessively or when they're slacking off doesn't encourage them. Praise should be a reward for effort and sometimes for results, not for laziness or sloppiness. If you're praising your kids and they haven't done anything to deserve it, what motivation do they have to work toward a goal? "Good job!" isn't appropriate if Johnny just cleaned his room by shoving all his dirty clothes in the corner! "Good try" isn't appropriate if Johnny just let the hockey puck pass through his legs!

Praise becomes excessive when parents give their kids an enthusiastic "way-to-go" for everything they do. But sometimes just acknowledging that your children have done something right without evaluating it can be just as effective. Instead of telling your son, "You got that math problem right. Fantastic! You're going to be the next Einstein!" try saying, "That's correct!" in an upbeat voice. That way, you won't oversaturate your child with praise but you do notice his accomplishments.

WE ALWAYS DEFER TO OUR KIDS.
The healthy way to make decisions is to compromise, taking into account both our feelings and our child's. But parents who overindulge tend to act as if their child's will is more important than their own. They always ask their kid, "What do you want to do?" before they've considered their own feelings. They often pride themselves on giving their child "a voice," but in reality, they're creating a mini tyrant. If Jonathan wants pizza on his mom's birthday, the family gets pizza. If Brianna doesn't want to go to Grandma's—or to church, or sometimes, even to school—she's allowed to stay at home.

SIGNS WE OVERCONTROL

WE'RE CONSTANTLY GETTING AFTER OUR CHILDREN.
Overcontrolling parents constantly lecture, critique, or push their kids. This is often subtle. Like when Brian is kicking a

beach ball around with his friends and his dad runs up and tells him, "You're kicking with your toe. You need to kick with the inside of your foot—like this." Although they only want to help their kids achieve their potential, these parents begin to over-teach, taking every opportunity to lecture and teach life lessons. As a result, they seldom spend time enjoying and playing with their children.

WE MAKE ALL THE DECISIONS.

When we have children, we are presented with countless decisions. What television shows will they watch? What kind of summer jobs will they have? Will they work while they're in school? Will they join the band or choir? If they're in the band, what instrument will they play? Will they try out for cross-country and follow in their dad's footsteps? What time should they go to bed? What chores should they do around the house? How much allowance will they get? What will their curfew be?

Decisions are a necessary part of life. But who makes them is a different issue. Parents who are overcontrolling tend to make all the decisions for their kids. They think they always know best, and because of that their children seldom get the opportunity to explore their own interests or passions.

This type of decision making extends to major life choices. One young adult told us, "I'm in medical school because it's something my parents have always wanted. The thing is, I don't know where I would be if I wasn't in medical school. I've never even had a chance to think about what I really want for my future."

WE'RE TOO UPTIGHT.

All kids need clear, firm rules and boundaries. Without them, they fail to flourish. But overcontrolling parents tend to make the entire relationship about right and wrong, good and bad. Sadly, this can color their relationship with God. Often they view spirituality simply in terms of "sin management," where they're constantly asking themselves, *Did I mess up? Is God mad at me? I hope He doesn't punish me.*

Many overcontrolling parents also find it difficult to relax or have fun. As one child said, "Every time we start to have a good time, my parents shut it down."

WE DON'T LET OUR KIDS EXPRESS THEMSELVES.

We all want our children to follow rules and not argue with adults. But our kids also need to learn how to express their feelings in respectful ways, and to learn the art of negotiation and problem solving. Overcontrolling parents can stifle emotional growth because they view a child's self-expression as disrespect or back talk. They often tell their kids, "What I say goes . . . End of story."

There is a time and place for absolute parental authority. Instead of shutting our kids down, though, we might ask, "Why should I let you go to the movie with Angie?" Or, "Why should I let you clean your room after lunch instead of this morning?" This teaches them how to use logic when they are upset—an important part of emotional growth.

WE PRY.

We all want to know what our kids think and feel. In some ways, wouldn't it be great if we could read their minds so we could edit out all the untruths and bad stuff? Parents who overcontrol, however, actually try to do this, prying into their kids' minds. They conduct machine-gun-style questioning after activities, saying, "Who did you talk to? What did she say? What did you say? Why did you do that?" They also read their children's notes, letters, and e-mails. Some parents will even eavesdrop on their kids' phone calls and rifle through their teenagers' drawers when they aren't home.

WE'RE MANIPULATIVE.

Some parents use guilt to control their kids. For instance, an overcontrolling father might tell his child, "You left your bike out and I had to pick it up with my bad back. You must want me to hurt myself!" When their kids don't do exactly what they want, these parents will say things like: "If you really loved me, you would . . ." "You're breaking your poor mother's heart." "You're ungrateful." "You're disrespectful." "You're a disappointment." They also undermine to make their children feel inadequate or unacceptable. "You never make good choices," they say. "You need me to help you."

They can withhold love, threatening to abandon their children if they're disobedient. For example, we've seen several parents tell their daughters, "If you marry him, I'll disown you!" This can also be subtle, such as when parents refuse to hug their kids when they do something wrong. The message is, "I will only love you if you do what I want."

WE SET UNREASONABLE EXPECTATIONS.

Overcontrolling parents expect too much. They want their kids to be the smartest, the funniest, and the strongest. Because of this, they don't give their children any latitude, picking out the best schools and sports equipment with the expectation that now that their kids have an edge, it's their responsibility to outperform their peers and meet their mom and dad's unrealistic goals.

REGAINING THE BALANCE

We're all sinful; we all make mistakes. Not one of us will achieve perfection until we get to heaven. The Bible acknowledges this, saying, "Now we see things imperfectly as in a poor mirror, but then we will see everything with perfect clarity. All that I know now is partial and incomplete, but then I will know everything completely, just as God knows me now" (1 Corinthians 13:12 NLT).

We want to help you develop an awareness of what toxic love looks like—not give you the ultimate guilt trip. If you're beginning to notice that you are overindulging, overprotecting, or overcontrolling your child, understand that *all* parents do these at some time, to varying extents. Bill Carmichael, author of *Habits of a Healthy Home* writes: "It has been painful for me in looking back to discover that I unconsciously did some things that fostered just the opposite of what I want to see in my children. I believe I am a good parent, but even good parents fail and foster the wrong environment."[1]

Our goal is not to eliminate controlling, indulging, and

protecting from your parenting style. We simply want to help you regain balance in how you show love to your kids. It can be very painful to look inward, so we want to encourage you to examine your relationship with your child without feeling guilty. Embrace the boundless mercy and grace that God gives us. There is no condemnation under Christ Jesus, only a call to grow and show Christlike love to others—especially our kids.

chapter three

Why We Love Too Much

The unexamined life is not worth living.

—Socrates

 $\mathcal{C}$ an you really love your child too much? The answer (again) is no. But that's a trick answer. Some parents exhibit behaviors that look like love but aren't, and others use loving behaviors in toxic amounts. That's what we really mean by "loving too much."

Why do we as parents love too much? There are dozens of reasons ranging from our own insecurity to our tendency to cling to the past. We've identified some of the most common reasons moms and dads overindulge, overprotect, or overcontrol. As you read, do your best to identify your own situation. Be honest with yourself—brutally so. By recognizing your mistakes, you'll be able to take the first step in creating a healthy love relationship with your child.

REASONS WE GIVE UNHEALTHY LOVE

WE FEEL OUT OF CONTROL.

Time and again, we hear parents say, "I just can't keep up with it all. And it makes me crazy when the kids are acting wild." Moms and dads who feel like their lives are out of control often respond by overcontrolling their children. Internally, these parents may be facing a host of worries and concerns, and believe that in order to keep a handle on things, they must spend all their energy and time organizing, planning, and obsessing. If you struggle with this kind of anxiety, your body may be tense, your muscles sore, and your mind tapped out.

Externally, these parents want everything neat and orderly—from their homes and cars, to their kids' closets, to their daily routines. When something gets messy or out of place, they get tense and anxious. And rather than giving their kids the grace to make mistakes and messes, overcontrolling parents instinctively clamp down on their children, hoping to gain some control in their own lives and to show the world that they are handling things just fine.

WE'RE DEALING WITH LOSS.

Have you seen the movie *Finding Nemo*? In it Nemo's father, the clown fish Marlin, loses his entire family to a predator—his wife and all his kids—except for his young son, Nemo. Several years later when Nemo goes missing, Marlin embarks on a desperate quest to find his only surviving child. As parents, it is easy to identify with Marlin. We feel his pain, and we feel it deeply.

There are a lot of Marlins in the world: parents who have suffered a major loss, such as the death of a spouse or a child, who safeguard their remaining children within an inch of their lives. These parents overprotect with gusto, keeping their kids from school and church activities, nixing sleepovers at friends' houses, monitoring their kids' every move with cell phones and beepers, treating their children like they're younger and more fragile than they really are.

In the movie, Marlin is dealing with *physical loss*. Physical loss occurs when we lose someone or something that is very important to us. On the other hand, *experience loss* occurs when we miss out on a significant experience or event—for instance, never having a father figure, healthy parent, or close family unit. Parents who have suffered physical loss often overprotect their children to prevent anything bad from happening, while parents who have dealt with experience loss may try to over-compensate for what they lacked growing up. If they grew up poor, living on government support and hand-me-downs, these moms and dads will shower their kids with only the best, most expensive toys and clothing. If their father was never around, they may cater to their kids' every whim and desire in an attempt to re-create the bonding experiences they never had.

WE'RE SCARED.

Fear is a strong motivator! When our children are sick, leaving for college, or getting married, it's easy to smother them out of fear that we'll lose them forever. Such fear can cause us to overprotect or overcontrol our children, sacrificing their growth and independence to shield them from real or imagined dangers. And it can drive us to overindulge our kids out of fear that if we teach them discipline and responsibility, they will only get mad or upset at us.

WE FEEL GUILTY.

Working too hard. Traveling too much. Missing important events. Tuning them out. It all boils down to not being there for our kids. As parents, nothing is more harrowing than realizing that we're drifting apart from our children. And nothing plagues us more with guilt.

That guilt eats at us like a cancer. Sadly, most parents we meet want to slow down and relax, focus on good deeds and charity, faith and family. They want to spend time with their kids—they know it's important! But they don't think they can. They're in too deep with work, school, or other commitments. As a result, these moms and dads will try to make up for their absence, compensating by not setting any rules or limits.[1] One father told us, "I work long hours so I can buy my kid things. And I buy my kid the best things because I feel so guilty for working such long hours!"

WE'RE TRYING TO FIX OUR PARENTS' MISTAKES.

Many parents vow to us, "I'll never treat my kids the way my parents treated me." But the reality is that family dynamics will often repeat themselves, despite our best intentions. We parent as we were parented, especially during times of stress. Why? Because it's familiar. It's what we know. If you were overcontrolled, you'll tend to control; treated harshly, you will parent harshly; overprotected, you'll protect too much; abused, you might abuse; overindulged, you'll probably indulge.

Other parents, overly cognizant of their parents' mistakes, may end up on the other end of the spectrum: if you were overprotected or overcontrolled as a child, you might become a laissez-faire, anything-goes parent; if you grew up in chaos, you might become overly restrictive.

WE FEEL LIKE WE MISSED OUT.

Dana and her three friends were sitting on the family room floor during her first slumber party when her mom, Lori, strolled into the room with two five-gallon tubs of ice cream. The girls giggled at the sight of the two buckets.

Dana's jaw dropped. "Mom . . . why so much ice cream?"

"Oh, you can never have too much ice cream—especially at a slumber party!" Lori replied. A moment later, she left the room and returned with two extra-large pepperoni pizzas, a duffle-bag-sized package of animal crackers, a surfboard-sized sheet cake, bags of assorted candies, party gifts for each girl, and seven DVDs.

"Mom," Dana exclaimed in embarrassment, "thanks, but there's no way we can eat all this! Why'd you get so much?"

Lori was actually meeting her own needs. As a child, she was poor. She wasn't allowed to have slumber parties because her parents couldn't afford ice cream and pizzas. When they finally did let her have a sleepover, they provided a half-eaten bag of potato chips. Lori wasn't going to let that happen to her daughter, so she brought home the entire store.

Maybe, like Lori, you are trying to make up for the past. Maybe you didn't make the football team. Or you failed in school. Or your family couldn't afford to send you away to college.

Parents who feel like they missed out are prone to loving too much. They dwell on missed opportunities and believe that as parents, they have a second chance to "do it right." Often they try to make up for the past by overcontrolling—grabbing each opportunity for their kids, whether their children want these golden "opportunities" or not. For example, dads who never got to play sports may push their kids to join every team or attend every sports camp possible in a quest to make them star players. They also may overindulge, giving their kids everything they never had.

When this happens, often the parents begin to live vicariously through their kids, seizing every moment as it unfolds for their children, sometimes becoming even more emotionally invested than their kids are. These parents try to be "friends" with their kids' friends. They park themselves on the floor of the family room all night during slumber parties, and they know the scoop on every kid in school. They call themselves active and involved parents, but they're really just trying to relive their own childhood.

WE WANT TO GIVE OUR KIDS THE UPPER HAND.

"Without a new computer, Taylor won't be able to take advantage of the latest educational programs. He'll be left behind. He won't have the leg up the other kids have." The idea of giving our kids everything to get ahead starts early. One parent we know began teaching his daughter to use a computer mouse when she was just eighteen months old. Another spent hundreds of dollars on educational flashcards and phonics DVDs to help her three-year-old get in to the right preschool.

From school supplies to sporting equipment, we've seen parents do just about anything to give their kids an edge. And while it's natural to want them to get ahead, we cannot emphasize enough that children are much more affected by the time they spend with their parents than by any high-tech, expensive toys money can buy.

WE'VE BEEN DUPED BY MARKETING.

How many times have you bought into the pressure of advertising, worrying that your son might feel "out of it" if he doesn't have the coolest (and, of course, most expensive) snowboard, or that your daughter will be the only girl on the block without the latest Hello Kitty® backpack? Marketing is no friend to parents! According to toy manufacturers and retail stores, there's no such thing as overindulgence. Children absolutely must have whatever it is that they're selling. And many parents buy into it.

One parent lamented to us, "Everything we buy for our kids these days requires other things, and it's not just batteries anymore! We can't just buy our daughter a Nintendo® for her birthday—we need to get her a game too. And we can't buy just one game, because it's a waste to get a new videogame system and have only one game. So we pick out two or three. Suddenly, we've gone from getting her one toy to purchasing an entire video library!"

Studies show kids spend on average twenty or more hours each week watching TV, more time than on any other activity besides sleeping.[2] That's not only way too much TV; that's a lot of commercials! With the barrage of advertising pressure, it's no wonder that we overindulge—especially when our children are telling us that "everybody else has one." (After all, they're probably right.) We feel better about ourselves when we can get McKenzie the latest designer shoes, or Kate a new computer, or Jack an updated Xbox the day it comes out.

WE'RE COMPENSATING FOR AN ABSENT PARENT.

When one parent is physically absent or emotionally unavailable, the other parent often worries that her child will grow up scarred from lack of attention. Unfortunately, this does happen. But rather than identifying healthy ways of helping their child—such as finding other positive role models for their son or daughter—some parents try to compensate by being too strict or far too protective. "I'm the only parent my kid has," they reason, "so I need to give him extra direction and extra protection. The buck stops with me!" Instead of making up for what their child is lacking, though, these parents often end up alienating their kids with their unreasonable rules.

WE'RE TRYING TO GET BACK AT OUR SPOUSE.

It happens every day. In a country where the divorce rate is nearing 50 percent, millions of parents are using their children as pawns in power struggles against their former spouse. Many of these parents, looking for ways to "get back" at their exes, will try to bond with their kids. This often leads to extreme overindulging as moms and dads focus on becoming buddies with their children, buying their love in an effort to win them over.[3] Other times they may become overcontrolling as they attempt to manipulate their kids into shunning the other spouse.

WE'RE NEEDY OR INSECURE.

One of our clients, Scott, grew up with an emotionally absent father and a stepmother who was often distracted with caring for her own demanding sons. Now as a dad with his own family, Scott was still battling feelings of neglect, pushing away his pain by focusing all his energy on overindulging his young daughter.

Many well-intentioned but needy parents such as Scott become overbearing when they try to ignore their own difficult past. Others end up overcontrolling, overprotecting, or overindulging in an effort to feel better about themselves. "If I've been a good parent," one mom told us, "then at least I've accomplished *something*."

These parents often make the mistake of trying to get love and satisfaction from their kids, oversaturating them with affection and gifts in the hopes that they will get that affection back tenfold. By overindulging, they cling to the hope that if they give their kids everything they want, their children will never abandon them. Many of these parents are single moms and dads or parents living in loveless marriages who desperately want to connect with someone and subconsciously place that emotional responsibility on their children.

They also tend to feed off their children's achievements, linking their kids' triumphs and failures to their own success as a parent. As a result, they have no tolerance for failure. "Today parents are turning their tots into trophies," Hara Estroff Marano wrote recently in *Psychology Today*—and they are sacrificing their children's developmental and psychological needs as a result.

If you find it difficult to let your kid be a kid, you may be steeped in this kind of vicarious living. Insecure about their own parenting, many upper-middle-class moms and dads have created an epidemic in our country as their kids' accomplishments become a litmus test for their own parenting success. Kids no longer have to till fields from dawn to dusk or toil in sooty factories, but more and more they are handed the burden of power lifting their parents' sense of self.[4]

TIME TO REFLECT

Now that you're familiar with some of the common reasons parents tend to "love too much," take a moment to reflect on your own state of mind. Are you running from a painful past?

Feeling out of control? Trying to make up for the childhood you never had?

Whatever the reasons, release them to God—let Him begin to work in your heart and mind. The Bible says, "If anyone is in Christ, he is a new creation; the old has gone, the new has come!" (2 Corinthians 5:17). Your heavenly Father knows both your imperfections and strengths. He can—and will—bring healing to your life, giving you the strength and wisdom to mend your relationship with your child.

chapter four

What's the Harm in Loving Too Much?

All a man's ways seem right to him,
but the LORD weighs the heart.

—Proverbs 21:2

*Y*our kids need you—in heavy doses! That means more than a day at the zoo or an evening at the baseball game, although that may be part of it. They want *you*. It's important. So if something inside tells you to draw closer to your kids, or to one of them in particular, take that as a word from the Holy Spirit.

If you're like most parents, you'll do just about anything to narrow the distance between you and your kids. As we leap into this section, you may be wondering, *What's the big deal if I love my kids too much?* Actually, we agree! It's important for you to indulge your kids now and then. Once in a while, all children need to feel like the whole world revolves around them. They need a day at the zoo when they get all the peanuts they want to feed the elephants—and eat too. They need a birthday where they get their favorite cake and ice cream. But if the world revolves around them every day, and they begin expecting their favorite cake Monday through Friday, or the moment they hit the zoo entrance they start whining about the peanuts, then the "specialness" has worn off and entitlement has arrived.

Like most things in life, too much of a good thing can simply be *too much*—whether it's indulging, controlling, or protecting our kids. Here, we've detailed some of the problems that arise when we love too much.

THE PITFALLS OF OVERPROTECTING

I (Tim) remember pushing my daughter Megan in her new pink Barbie racecar. I'm not sure what I was thinking. After all, if you have hard plastic wheels, a steeply sloped driveway, and a push from Dad, things can get out of control fast. And they did. Before I knew it, Megan was shooting down the hill straight toward the road—and I couldn't keep up with her. I was terrified. At the last possible moment I dove for the car. Somehow, with my chin down in the asphalt, I managed to grab the rear of the car and shove it—and Megan—into some shrubs. You'd think Megan would have been sobbing, but she was screaming for joy! She thought it was the best ride ever. Meanwhile, I felt like I'd had open-heart surgery.

If our kids are crossing into harm's way, we'll do anything to help them! That's natural and healthy. But what if I had been so shaken by the incident that I decided never to let Megan play outside or ride her bike again? In that instance, I may have felt as if I were coming to Megan's aid, but that "aid" would actually be stripping my daughter of responsibility. She would never learn to bike or play safely on her own.

Need more examples? Overprotected kids seldom get to play in the McDonald's Playland because they might pick up germs, or make mud pies because they'll get dirty, or ride their scooter because they might fall and skin their knees.

Parents who overprotect believe they're being good, careful parents. They pride themselves on being informed of every hazard or potential problem. Unfortunately, this kind of protection can cause kids to have some of the following problems:

THEY LACK DISCIPLINE.

Adults who were overprotected may lack discipline and social responsibility. They can be self-centered and unable to negotiate or resolve conflict with others. Sometimes people who were overprotected as children may even grow up to believe that they are "above the law" in respect to government and God.

THEY BECOME UNDERACHIEVERS.

Overprotected children tend to trail in personal, spiritual, and social development.[1] They often become underachievers—after all, what's the point of trying to accomplish something if mom and dad are always there to handle things for you? When that happens, they fail to thrive emotionally, never reaching their potential.

THEY BECOME DEPENDENT.

Rather than growing up to be independent, these kids typically become insecure, unable to face life's challenges with confidence or to make important decisions without direction from another person.[2] They want someone else to be in charge. An overprotected child in his thirties might still depend on his mom and dad for money and other essentials, periodically moving back home.

We've also seen many overprotected kids cling desperately to unhealthy, controlling, and potentially abusive relationships. These kids become doormats, letting others make decisions while they sit quietly, hoping no one gets upset with them.

THEY HAVE TROUBLE REGULATING THEIR EMOTIONS.

We all know people who whine bitterly when they get the slightest cold or complain constantly when something doesn't go their way. It's easy to laugh at these people, but we shouldn't—their situation is sad. Unfortunately, when parents shelter their kids from the world's hardships, their children often become high maintenance. It's not that these children can't handle their own feelings; they simply don't have the practice. So when they get uncomfortable, they'll seek out any-thing to numb their pain—turning to things like shopping, alco-hol, drugs, sex, violence, and food.

They're immature.

Impulsive and self-indulgent, overprotected children believe the world revolves around them. Because they've never been able to make their own decisions, they don't know how to exer-cise discernment. Such kids grow up spending money foolishly, have trouble holding down a job, and seldom take responsibili-ty for the ongoing needs of their family.

Another area these children struggle with is loyalty—first with friends and later in their marriages. Since they never learn how to handle life's challenges, they aren't inclined to be faithful to their spouse when the going gets tough. They may wander, looking for the fictional spouse who won't cause any conflict.

Overindulging . . . at What Price?

Many parents we counsel struggle to understand the problem with overindulging their kids—especially in today's world, where it seems every child has a closet full of clothes, a box full of toys, and a garage full of equipment. After all, showering your kids with gifts and "stuff" is just part of being a parent, right? Even Jesus says that loving your children involves pro-viding them good things: "If you . . . know how to give good gifts to your children, how much more will your Father in heaven give good gifts to those who ask him!" (Matthew 7:11).

But overindulging is really just trying to buy your kids' love. And love isn't really about "things." In fact, despite all their material blessings, overindulged kids often become angry, resentful adults. This shocks their parents, who were sure that all those years of sacrifice would turn their kids into gracious, happy people. Other common characteristics of overindulged children include:

THEY ARE SELFISH.

Adults who were overindulged may be very "me" focused, lacking empathy,[3] respect, and tolerance for others. They tend to have poor social skills and tact, and throw tantrums or make scenes when they're dissatisfied.[4] They have trouble realizing when "enough is enough" in regard to talking, teasing, joking, or loving, unwittingly intruding on others' time and personal boundaries.

Parents of overindulged children often complain about how their kids don't respect them when they're talking with another adult. They frequently interrupt, and when they are scolded for doing so, they say matter-of-factly, "Well, I wanted to say something."

THEY HAVE LITTLE SENSE OF ACCOMPLISHMENT.

Children who are used to getting everything they want never learn the benefits of hard work. Because they think that significance and happiness come from material things, they derive very little satisfaction and meaning from their accomplishments.[5] And because they haven't had to persevere or complete goals, they rarely stick with things long enough to be successful. (Oddly, the one exception is with video games. These kids will often play video games until they have mastered them.)

THEY LACK SELF-CONTROL.

When parents are too permissive, letting their kids do whatever they want, their children never learn how to stay within healthy limits. Because they haven't had enough wise and loving guidance from their moms and dads, they often become self-destructive by acting out, getting poor grades, using drugs and alcohol, becoming sexually promiscuous, and even developing anxiety disorders.

THEY HAVE A SENSE OF ENTITLEMENT.

With both their needs and their wishes being met, overindulged children often feel they "deserve" to get what they want. This can create dire ramifications for future relationships. For example, few newlywed husbands can afford to spend on their wife what she received when she was supported by daddy. Christy was an only child. A very indulged child of well-to-do parents. She never wanted for a thing. Her parents raised her to be gracious and kind. All was well, they thought, until she married Gary. Although Gary was successful for his age, he couldn't afford her the lifestyle to which she was accustomed. He loved her, but didn't treat her like a princess. Christy had such a sense of entitlement that she soon resented Gary for what he couldn't provide. Her parents' overindulgent love cost their daughter her future love.

THE COST OF OVERCONTROL

Overcontrolling parents often restrict their kids' growing sense of self through criticism—often cloaked as corrective feedback—about friends, music, hobbies, interests, grades . . . everything. They also stifle their children's emotions, quashing dissenting opinions and the expression of feelings like anger and sadness. Their biggest concern is instilling obedience.

These parents fail to see that they can empower their kids simply by accepting them as unique and valuable individuals. Although they may mean well, overcontrolling parents can cause lifelong damage to their kids. As children, a few are happy to let their mom and dad make the decisions, but most kids who are overcontrolled eventually rebel. Research shows that adults who have been overcontrolled sometimes harbor great anger and resentment toward their parents, battling relentless bouts of pain and humiliation. Some turn to substance abuse to numb these emotions, while others compensate by overcontrolling their own children. The most common problems include the following.

THEY HAVE PROBLEMS WITH INTIMACY AND RELATIONSHIPS.

People who have been constantly critiqued and monitored expect way too much of themselves and others. So when they try to build close relationships, major problems can occur. They wonder, *What if we're not happy? What if we can't meet each other's needs?*

Also, when kids grow up under a parent's critical eye, they expect the same criticism and rejection from others, so they tend to hold back their feelings in relationships. They may desperately want to build close friendships and romantic relationships, but they can't shake the gnawing feeling that as soon as they drop the mask and let themselves be vulnerable, they'll be criticized.

THEY BLAME THEMSELVES FOR EVERYTHING.

Overcontrolling parents (often inadvertently) impress on their kids that if everything isn't going just right, it's probably because they messed things up or failed. This blaming creates deep long-term wounds, causing them to take responsibility for things they shouldn't.

THEY PRETEND TO COMPLY.

Some children may act as if they're listening to their parents and adhering to their morals, standards, and advice, but in reality they are living double lives. These kids may act like perfect, responsible angels, but as soon as their parents turn their backs, they are sneaking out of the house to party with their friends. As one frustrated parent told us, "I've trained my child to become sneaky."

THEY BECOME PASSIVE AGGRESSIVE.

Other children put up with their parents' overcontrolling behavior because they find it too difficult to reject all their parents' demands. Though this compromise helps to keep the peace, there's always tension between the frustrated child who seems to be "dragging his feet" and the angry parent who feels "half listened to." These children are experts at procrastinating, sulking, and dawdling. They don't usually talk back, but they can be sarcastic and resentful.

THEY WORRY TOO MUCH ABOUT WHAT OTHER PEOPLE THINK.

Overcontrolled kids are affirmed by what they do rather than who they are. As one teen explained to us, "You're only as good as your last dance." In order to feel accepted, they naturally try to seek the approval and praise of others, even to their detriment.

Many of the kids we meet are extremely fearful of disapproval and rejection. They may intensely dread being in social situations where they might do something to embarrass themselves. The smallest things—even harmless teasing or gentle suggestions—will make them bristle or tear up. They read into benign comments and spend hours obsessing about whether they have offended somebody or done something stupid in front of others. Constantly fearful, they can get locked into a chronic mode of social avoidance.

THEY HAVE TROUBLE RELAXING OR HAVING FUN.

Overcontrolled kids are allowed little time for fun or leisure, and they carry this attitude into adulthood. Since they are rarely taught the value of having fun or appreciating the moment, these children can be very driven. They're unhappy if they don't get straight A's, and they look at every sport and extracurricular activity as a competition or simply filler for their college resume. As adults, they don't take vacations, and they work around the clock.

LETTING GO

Dozens of research studies along with our own experience reveal the dangers associated with overprotecting, overindulging, and overcontrolling. When we love too much, we emotionally handicap our children, and these handicaps follow them far into adulthood. But such measures usually aren't necessary! Kids are amazingly capable and resilient. They learn from failure, are encouraged by success, and keep going when they face challenges. It's up to us to let go of our tendencies and let our kids live.

part two

Healthy Love

LOVING YOUR CHILD
TOO MUCH

chapter five

The Right Way to Love

Be imitators of God, therefore, as dearly loved children and live a life of love, just as Christ loved us and gave himself up for us as a fragrant offering and sacrifice to God.

—Ephesians 5:1–2

*C*hristy brought her thirteen-year-old daughter, Claudia, to see us, because she was concerned about Claudia's poor behavior and attitude. We began our session by talking about their latest conflict: Christy had not let Claudia go to the movies with her friends that weekend.

"Claudia hadn't made a dent in her homework," Christy explained to us. "She spent all day listening to music in her room instead of researching her science-fair project. I told

Claudia she had to stay home and make some headway on her assignment."

Claudia crossed her arms and rolled her eyes at her mother.

Suddenly, the dynamic changed. "Don't do that to me, young lady!" Christy shrieked, wagging her finger at her daughter. "You don't disrespect your mother like that! I don't care if we are in a counseling session or anywhere, you don't do that to me—*ever*! I'm sick and tired of your trashy, filthy attitude and your petty, snotty remarks."

Claudia stared at the wall, biting her lip.

After a moment, we turned to her and asked, "Claudia, would you like to respond? How does that make you feel?"

Claudia glared at her mother, refusing to speak. Several minutes went by until she broke down crying and buried her head in her hands. We gave her a break and let her leave the office.

After Claudia left—and Christy had calmed down—we asked her how she felt about the incident. "Well, I think she needs to know that you don't disrespect your parents," Christy said. "The Bible says you need to honor your father and mother."

"Yes," we agreed, "it's very important for children to learn respect. But do you feel that the way you responded to *her* was respectful?"

"I don't know, and I really don't care," Christy snapped. "She needed to learn a lesson, and I was teaching it to her. You can't be rude and disrespectful to your parents and not suffer the consequences."

"Was your response to her—the raising of your voice, the

remarks you made to her, your tone of voice—the consequence for her disrespect?" we ventured.

"Absolutely!" she said boldly. "That's what you get when you disrespect your parents. When I was a kid, my mother would have smacked me upside the head if I'd rolled my eyes at her. But we can't do that these days. That's the reason kids are the way they are. You can't discipline them the way they really need it."

Christy was partly right—one of the most important facets of parenting is teaching our kids to follow our rules, and that includes respecting authority (see Exodus 20:12). Unfortunately, like many overcontrolling parents we meet, Christy thought her top priority needed to be instilling her values in her daughter, focusing all her attention on Claudia's misconduct. As we attempted to explain to Christy, *how* we train our children to walk in Christ's footsteps is just as important as *what* we train them.

All the Bible memory verses and Sunday school lessons, rules and guidelines, and bedtime prayers and lectures will be ineffective if we don't model for our children how to give and receive God's love. And that starts with the way we first love them.

PARENTING BY THE GOLDEN RULE

Jesus was no stranger to people who focused on rules and discipline to the exclusion of love and relationships. The Pharisees and Sadducees, the most powerful religious leaders of His day, put all their energy into keeping every detail of

God's commands. So when these leaders asked Jesus what the greatest commandment of all was, they must have been shocked when He responded, "'Love the Lord your God with all your heart and with all your soul and with all your mind.' This is the first and greatest commandment. And the second is like it: 'Love your neighbor as yourself.' All the Law and the Prophets hang on these two commandments" (Matthew 22:37–40).

As Jesus explained, God's entire law rests on the principle of love: loving God and loving your neighbor as yourself. With that in mind, we believe "training" our kids is about preparing them to love and be loved. But what does healthy Christlike love look like, and how do we apply it to our relationship with our children?

We begin with respect. As the scenario with Christy and Claudia illustrates, we can't expect our kids to respect us if we don't offer them that same respect and love. Scripture tells us that Jesus, who is our model for perfect love, does this for us: "We love because he first loved us" (1 John 4:19). But Christy was giving her daughter what we like to call "eye-for-an-eye respect." (Actually, it was more like head-for-an-eye in that she was doling out much more disrespect than her daughter was.) In effect, she was saying, "I'll treat you the way you treat me. If you disrespect me, I'll disrespect you." Of course, most parents who teach this philosophy don't realize what they're doing. They think they're simply disciplining their children.

Like them, Christy was unaware just how destructive her method of discipline was. At best, it would teach her daughter not to disrespect her outwardly, but Claudia would never truly respect her mother in her heart. They would never develop a healthy, loving relationship. The only lesson Christy was teaching Claudia was to treat people exactly as they treated her. And Claudia was a fast learner!

Instead of measuring out to your kids the same amount of attitude, love, and affection they give you, try to follow what we call the Golden Rule of Parenting: treat your child the way that you want to be treated. For one, this is a more biblical approach (see Matthew 7:12). It can be hard to follow too. It dictates that no matter how poorly your children are behaving, you will repay them with love and respect.

You might be thinking, *Are you saying that if I want to show God's love to my child, I can't administer consequences for his behavior?* Of course not! That would be just as destructive as spewing unkind words and disrespect. It is possible to respectfully provide discipline and consequences. For example, when a judge sentences someone for breaking the law, she doesn't say, "You filthy, no-good criminal!" Instead, she tells the defendant, "Mr. Smith, you are found guilty of willingly breaking a law. You are being sentenced to probation and a two-hundred-dollar fine. You may see the clerk outside the courtroom. Have a good day." See the difference?

By following the Golden Rule of Parenting, we can begin to build the foundation for a healthy love relationship with our child. This is absolutely essential—without a solid, biblical foundation, trying to "fix" our tendencies to overcontrol, overindulge, or overprotect will be fruitless.

OTHER ELEMENTS OF BIBLICAL LOVE

The Bible offers other good advice for loving our children. In his letter to the church at Ephesus, the apostle Paul gave the following instructions: "Children, obey your parents in the Lord, for this is right. 'Honor your father and mother'—which is the first commandment with a promise—'that it may go well with you and that you may enjoy long life on the earth.'" Then he turned his focus, saying, "Fathers, do not exasperate your children; instead, bring them up in the training and instruction of the Lord'" (Ephesians 6:1–4).

Paul could have just instructed children to obey their parents. But he also addressed parents, telling fathers to look at their own hearts and acknowledge the way their actions affect their kids—a challenge that we believe applies to both parents.

As with Jesus' greatest commandment, Paul's guidelines for relationships remind us that we need to take responsibility for loving our children before we can expect to train and mold them. Specifically, we must not "exasperate"—provoke or anger them. This is so important that Paul mentions it in two different books of the Bible: first in this passage from Ephesians, and also in the book of Colossians (3:20–21).

What are some of the most common things we do to upset our kids? We've outlined them here:

WE SHOW FAVORITISM.

Ask any son or daughter who the favorite child is in their family, and you'll probably get an answer. Sibling favoritism is offensive and hurtful, and often leads to feelings of inferiority, anger, resentment, and bitterness. The biblical story of twins Esau and Jacob is a prime example of how favoritism can damage a family. We learn in the book of Genesis that the boys' father, Isaac, preferred Esau, while their mother, Rachel, favored Jacob. This led to deceit between the parents, and to Jacob stealing Esau's birthright and blessing.

We neglect them.

Second Samuel 14–17 tells the story of David and his son Absalom, who were estranged and bitter enemies for many years as a result of David's neglectful parenting and refusal to address important, hurtful family problems. When his son sinned, King David drove him out of the kingdom, refusing to see Absalom. Later, Absalom temporarily took over his father's kingdom and almost had David killed.

It's our job as parents to be involved with our kids and teach them to manage their sin and emotions like anger, frustration, discouragement, and sorrow. When we create a loving and close relationship with our kids, we are able to chart a positive course to navigate future challenges. Without this affection and approval, our kids will grow up to be resentful and hurt.

We control or protect too much.

As we've already illustrated, overprotecting or overcontrolling is unnecessary and harmful. Be careful not to smother your child. Teach him or her how to live and make independent choices.

We try to live their lives for them.

Many parents are guilty of trying to recover from their losses and failures by living vicariously through their children. In doing so, they might push their kids into sports, studies, and occupations that leave little room for the children to explore their own God-given talents.

We're discouraging.

"Why can't you hit the ball?" "You're such a klutz." "That's my little airhead!" Comments like these, even made in jest, will echo in our kids' ears so loudly they'll continue into adulthood.

Paul wrote, "Fathers, do not embitter your children, or they will become discouraged" (Colossians 3:21). Discouragement instills a negative, broken spirit. Instead of critiquing or teasing your kids, make a list that says what you like about each of your children and share it with them.

Following in His Footsteps

As God's children and ambassadors here on earth, our primary function is to spread His gospel so that eventually the whole world knows Him. Nowhere is our responsibility to bring people to Christ more acute than within our own families. Fortunately, once we've identified and have begun to correct our mistakes, we'll find that our children are much more receptive to our instruction and wisdom. We've listed four ways parents might accomplish this holy work:

TRAINING THROUGH EXAMPLE

My (Tim) daughter Megan loves to write, draw, and express her creative side. My son Zach also loves to draw (he started out early on the walls!). What's interesting is that many times the picture that children "draw" of their parents is very similar to the picture they have of God. As a parent, what example do you give your children? When they think of you, what type of picture do they draw? Believe us, your kids will notice if you say one thing and then do another. The foundation of effective parenting is your own godly lifestyle.

TRAINING THROUGH INSTRUCTION

Your kids absorb everything you do—especially when they're young. If your favorite color is red, your daughter's favorite color will be red. If you like the Steelers, your son will be their biggest fan. But our influence extends farther than that. As parents, we have the God-given responsibility to instruct our kids in the ways of the LORD (Deuteronomy 6:6–9; Proverbs 4). Through both our words and actions, we teach them not only how to bake cookies, catch a ball, drive a car, or train a dog but also how to pray, persevere, trust, and reach out.

TRAINING THROUGH DISCIPLINE

Kids need structure and boundaries, and they are notorious for pushing to see how far those rules can be stretched! When we engage in healthy discipline, we provide a tremendous opportunity for learning. Discipline teaches our kids right from wrong, and it opens up the channels of communication with them.

Many parents we meet are so busy with work and other commitments that they overindulge—because they feel guilty about their absence, they just want to be nice and have a good time with their kids. Be wary of trying to be the "fun" parent. Good parents enjoy their kids, but they also teach boundaries and self-control.

Training Through Love

It bears repeating: what your children need and want isn't a great new toy—it's you. Aside from telling your kids how much you love them, live out your love daily by taking them to basketball practice, piano recitals, and swim lessons; eating their pancakes and mini pizzas; holding their hands; kissing their noses; finding out what's important to them; laughing with them; crying together; and most importantly, showing them how to love God and others.

The Fruit of Christlike Love

How do we know if we're truly showing our kids God's love and training them to walk in His footsteps? Balanced, Christlike love produces qualities that promote spiritual health, happiness, and success. With it, our kids develop the following strong and godly virtues:

- A Christ-centered attitude
- Moral discernment
- A sense of humor
- Patience
- The ability to endure pain
- Personal and spiritual growth
- The ability to forgive and accept forgiveness
- Problem-solving skills
- Character that is slow to anger
- Resilience
- Communication skills
- Respect for others
- Compassion
- Responsibility
- Courage
- Self-confidence
- Empathy
- Self-control
- Gratitude
- Self-discipline
- Integrity
- Self-respect

- Kindness

- Spiritual discernment

- Love for life and learning

- Tolerance

When we create a foundation of Christlike love, we can build a healthy, more intimate relationship with our kids—one that does not overindulge, overprotect, or overcontrol.

When they are loved but not overindulged, kids will learn:

- It's okay to feel what I do, be it anger or frustration or love, but I have the responsibility to express my feelings in a godly way. I can feel strong emotions and still make good choices.

- It is okay to want things, but I understand I don't need to have everything I want.

- I am accountable for my actions.

- There is joy in earning things instead of always being given things.

When they are loved but not overcontrolled, kids will learn:

- My parents respect my choices, though they don't always agree with them.

- I know who I am, and I am responsible for my own decisions.

- I, with God's blessing, am in control of my own destiny.

- With God's help I can deal with difficult decisions and choices.
- I know my likes and dislikes.

When they are loved but not overprotected, kids will learn:
- I don't like being disappointed, but I can learn from it.
- Life can be painful, but through God's grace, I can find joy.
- The world can be a dangerous place, but generally it is not that dangerous.
- I am capable of giving and receiving love.

chapter six

The Three R's of Healthy Love

Train a child in the way he should go, and when he is old
he will not turn from it.

—Proverbs 22:6

Back-talking. Arguing. Not listening. Being disrespectful. Being stubborn. Fighting. Cursing. As counselors, we hear these complaints every day from parents who are tired of their kids' bad behavior. And as parents, you've probably gotten tired of hearing how to fix that bad behavior: "Try a sticker program." "Bribe her." "Be tougher . . . Have you tried a good spanking? What about using time-outs?" "He just needs attention." "Leave him alone; he's going through a difficult phase." "She'll grow out of it."

Many parenting programs teach parents flashy discipline techniques—elaborate sticker programs, one-two-three time-outs, behavioral charts, mystery bags, punishments like making children run and do callisthenic exercises . . . The list goes on and on. These programs help parents become better at enforcing the rules, teaching them how to be more clear, consistent, and immediate in handling their child's misbehavior.

These programs can be useful, but they focus almost exclusively on the rules rather than the relationship. For many moms and dads, this is appealing. Parents have told us, "I'm willing to change the way I act toward him *after* he gets rid of that attitude and starts behaving himself!" The problem with this approach is it assumes that if you change your child's behavior through discipline, your relationship with him or her will improve. The truth is it works the other way around! Good behavior is anchored by a strong, loving relationship.

NO SIMPLE SOLUTIONS

In our practice, we teach parents the three R's of parenting: rules, relationship, and respect. Our philosophy is, rules with relationship lead to respect, but rules without relationship lead to rebellion.

One family we saw for a consultation was having a terrible time with their eight-year-old son, Kendall. They had been seeing two counselors—a husband and wife team—for several months about Kendall's temper tantrums, backtalk, and rude and obnoxious behavior toward his brothers and sisters. The counselors told the parents to "get tough" with Kendall, using a regimented program of spanking and time-outs.

His parents were a little uneasy with this approach. It created a lot of tension in the household. If Kendall refused to pass the ketchup at dinner, a major battle ensued.

To make matters worse, the counselors told the parents they should avoid working on their relationship with Kendall until he stopped throwing tantrums and back-talking for at least two weeks. Why? They said any warmth would only reinforce his negative behavior!

Needless to say, the program failed miserably. Kendall was soon suspended from school for fighting. When his parents complained that he was also getting worse at home, their counselors explained: "You haven't been tough enough. Obviously you've been getting soft with him." That's when they decided to come to us.

This example may seem a bit extreme. Few licensed professionals would offer such severe advice. But some of them do teach that rules are at the heart of parenting. This idea puts the cart before the horse! The path begins with winning your child's heart and building a strong relationship. It's not easy, and it requires God's help for strength and stamina, but often the trails with the best views are uphill.

THE POWER OF RELATIONSHIPS

Most people fail to understand the power of relationships. A good friend, philosopher, and theologian used to call our method "thumb sucking," because he believed that focusing on relationships was like coddling a baby. Even psychological researchers once thought that what you did in the context of close relationships had very little impact on your brain. But thanks to recent breakthroughs in brain imaging, neuroscientists can now see how our brain works when we're sad, angry, at peace, and when we're having a deep conversation with a loved one. These images show that the brain is powerfully affected by relationships![1]

We've outlined five key elements of a positive relationship:

EMPATHY

Empathy is the ability to understand how another person feels, to see what it's like to be in her skin. It doesn't mean you have to agree with her beliefs or even her perspectives. It simply means you understand her and are able to communicate that understanding to the other person. Empathy is one of the most powerful qualities of a close relationship. It actually unlocks the brain's natural calming chemicals, making it physically reassuring to feel understood by another person.[2]

Part of building a relationship with our kids is communicating to them that what they think and feel is important and that we take their concerns seriously. God does this with us. Scripture says, "The LORD your God is with you, he is mighty to save. He will take great delight in you, he will quiet you with his love, he will rejoice over you with singing" (Zephaniah 3:17).

Still, many parents have trouble showing empathy to their children because they worry that it will jeopardize their authority. Fortunately, we can validate our kids' feelings without giving up any power or authority. For example, we might say: "I know you don't like that rule—it really makes you mad." "I know your sister gets under your skin." "I know you get frustrated when you do your homework, because you'd rather be out playing . . . I felt the same way as a kid." Each of these statements offers validation without sacrificing authority.

Using empathy with our kids will help them calm down and deal with strong feelings. It's also the first step in getting them to listen to what we have to say!

ASSERTIVENESS

Assertiveness is respectfully expressing your feelings and perspectives. When you assert, it's best to be straightforward and factual, not blaming and critical. Don't exaggerate your points. And try to show empathy.

It's important for children to understand how you feel about their behavior, so be specific. For example, I (Gary) will say to my son, "Jacob, I know you don't like doing homework and you'd much rather be playing Playstation®, but our rule is that you can't play Playstation until your homework is done." The basic idea is that you set limits in a way that is clear, respectful, and empathizes with your child's perspective.

RESPECT

"Respect your elders." "Listen to your teacher." "Say please and thank you." "Be nice to your sister!" How often do we say these things to our kids? Ironically, most people don't really understand how to teach their children respect.

But kids learn respect through our example. They see how we treat our spouse. Our friends. Our parents. And even the customer service representative at the home improvement store.

They also notice how we treat them. Children tend to treat people the way they are treated. Many parents we meet demand respect from their kids and dish out just the opposite. As we explained earlier, if we want to develop a positive, loving relationship with our children, we need to follow the Golden Rule of Parenting and treat them with the same respect we require from them.

WARMTH

Warmth is an emotional tone. You can hear it in someone's voice and see it in her facial expression and body language. It conveys the message, "I like you," "I want to spend time with you," "I want to hear what you have to say," and "I value you." You probably know people who lack warmth. Even if they don't mean to, they send the message, "I don't like you," or "I don't have time for you."

Many parents don't realize what kind of emotional tone they use with their children—especially parents who overcontrol. In counseling, we sometimes film parents' interactions with their kids and play back the film for them. As we watch, we ask them to rate their emotional tone. This is very difficult to do, especially if you have a challenging child. For instance, parents of hyperactive children frequently have frowns on their faces, clinched jaws, and tense posture. But children can sense this kind of negativity, which leads them to become even more anxious and hyperactive. This is endlessly frustrating to parents. Since they never realized what kind of tone they were projecting, their attempts to fix their negative behavior feel futile.

There are practical ways, though, to use positive attention and warmth to help improve your child's behavior. These methods, which we'll explore in chapter 11, are similar to the way grace works in the lives of Christians. Under grace, we transform our sinful behavior into obedient living, motivated by a desire to please God.

RESPONSIVENESS

Responsive parents understand that each of their kids is different. God created us all as unique individuals—for a purpose (see Ephesians 4:11–13)! Several years ago, I (Gary) had a passing conversation with a group of moms who had already raised their children and were now enjoying being grandmothers. As we talked, I expressed how important it is for parents to make adjustments in their parenting style to fit each child's needs.

One young mother overheard our conversation and said, "But this book I'm reading says you should get your child onto the schedule they provide and that you shouldn't make adjustments."

"Honey," one of the grandmothers replied, "I had to learn this lesson very early, and you should too: each of your kids is different. What works for one doesn't necessarily work for the other. Kids are not one-size-fits-all."

Take Action

Your relationship with your kids is at the heart of parenting. Of course, what that relationship looks like may be different with each child, depending on his or her needs and your own tendencies toward unhealthy love.

Overindulging parents tend to focus only on their relationship with their kids to the exclusion of setting rules. Meanwhile, overcontrolling and overprotecting moms and dads usually view parenting as a series of dos and don'ts. How good their relationship is with their kids depends on how well their kids are following the rules.

Of course, as we've seen, you must be just as committed to maintaining a strong, nurturing relationship as you are to setting clear boundaries and enforcing limits. In the next three chapters we'll explore each style of unhealthy love and look at some practical ways to avoid it.

chapter seven

Loving Without Overindulging

Look at the lilies and how they grow.
They don't work or make their clothing.

—Matthew 6:28 (NLT)

*E*very year Ron and Carol do their best to make their son's birthday better than the year before. When he turned ten, Ron Jr. got all the techno-gadgets he asked for, a bag of football equipment, and a closet full of new clothes. And that year, just like every other, Ron and Carol watch their son open his massive array of gifts only to toss them aside and run out to play with old toys.

With action figures stacked in mountains at the local toy store, videogames so real you could practically crawl inside the monitor, and the never-ending chorus of your kids shrieking, "But so-and-so has one!" sometimes it's easier to just cave in and buy your children what they want. After all, won't it make them feel happy and loved? And isn't that what parenting is all about?

Countless parents who struggle with spoiling their kids have told us, "I grew up poor, and I don't want my child to have to go 'without' like I did!" Although they mean well, these parents believe—incorrectly—that the only way their child won't go without is to give him everything they can. There's a world of difference, however, between having a child who "goes without" and having one who doesn't get everything he wants, or *thinks* he wants.

We all love to see the look on our kids' faces when they get something new. But that look doesn't last, and kids' hearts become empty as their rooms fill with dust-covered "stuff." Finally coming to grips with that, Ron and Carol decided on a new approach for Ron Jr.'s birthday this year—fewer gifts and more family. They spent the day together having a picnic, visiting the zoo, and instead of buying an expensive store-bought ice cream cake, they all made Ron's birthday cake the night before. At the picnic, just before cake and ice cream, Ron Jr. opened his gifts—games the whole family could enjoy with him. Then when they returned home, they gathered on the couch to watch a movie.

Ron Jr. ended up hugging and kissing both his parents and thanking them for "the best birthday ever." Ron and Carol certainly liked Ron Jr.'s reaction, but they loved the fact that their day together helped build a closer relationship with their son.

As Ron and Carol learned, kids may say they want material

things, but what they really need—and want—is their parents' attention. Remember, parents, you shouldn't be trying to buy your children's memories; by fostering a good relationship with them, you become their memories!

AN EFFORTLESS CHILDHOOD

Overindulging parents don't just give their kids too many material gifts—they also give them an effortless childhood, one with too few limits and not enough responsibility. They believe their children should have everything their hearts' desire without having to earn it, and they don't want their kids to have to endure any of the hardships associated with normal life. These kids never clean their rooms, and have never washed the dishes or mowed the lawn. And if they do any kind of work, it's usually because they've been bribed.

What these parents don't realize is that chores are not only important for teaching responsibility, they're also good for kids' self-esteem. We've found that kids generally enjoy helping their parents with the household chores—even when they say the opposite. If Lexi helps out the next time you paint the bathroom or landscape the front yard, she'll develop a sense of ownership and achievement whenever she sees the finished product. She'll know she made a useful contribution.

Kids need the love and support of their parents. They need their parents to be there for them, even to help bail them out from time to time. But if their parents require nothing from them, give them everything they want, and are always around to clean up their "messes"—at school, with friends, and sometimes even with the police—they'll never learn personal responsibility.

When Dayton was growing up, his mom followed him around the house, picking up the trail of debris he left behind—pajamas in the upstairs hallway, breakfast crumbs on the family room coffee table, books in the foyer, school clothes wadded up in his bedroom. There were food, toys, and wrappers everywhere.

She thought she was making his life a little easier. But now, at thirty-one, Dayton still leaves his trash behind him, and the people he shares an office with are not so accommodating. Not only that, but his work is as sloppy as his desk. "Why is he always such a mess?" Dayton's coworkers whisper to each other. "Doesn't he care?"

Like Dayton's mom, most parents who overindulge have good intentions. But those good intentions can cause major repercussions. For instance, in a study that interviewed adults who were overindulged as children, not one of the participants said they were happy about having been spoiled. Though they believed that their parents meant well, they resented the fact that they had been given a silver-spoon childhood. Because of it, they had trouble making decisions, completing household chores, or raising their own kids. One researcher said, "The more they were overindulged, the less they saw themselves as effective people."[1]

Overindulging can also cause spiritual damage. God calls Christians to set their eyes on spiritual things, not material things (see 2 Corinthians 4:18). Specifically, the Bible says, "Keep your lives free from the love of money and be content with what you have, because God has said, 'Never will I leave you; never will I forsake you'" (Hebrews 13:5). If we shower our children with "things" or allow them to avoid paying the consequences for their sin or misbehavior, we are putting their focus on earthly rewards—good feelings and material possessions—rather than spiritual riches.

ARE YOU SPOILING?

Many parents know they are overindulging, but they continue to give in because it's easier than putting their foot down. Other parents overindulge without realizing it, giving in because they have trouble distinguishing between overindulgence and the occasional treat. Take a minute to reflect and see if you've been giving or doing too much:

- Does my indulging keep my kids from learning values or discipline?
- "Don't get a job. I'll increase your allowance."
- "I'll just give you one of the binders from work—they won't notice."
- "The maid will clean that up."
- Could my indulging harm my child?
- "Here, I'll do your math homework for you."
- "Sure, you can have fast food for dinner every night."
- Does my indulging excessively deplete the family resources?

- "We can't really afford it, but . . ."
- "I had to skip work and leave the house a mess to do this for you!"
- Does my indulging meet my needs instead of my child's?
- "Aren't I a great mom?"
- "I give 100 percent to my kids, don't you?"
- "This is proof that I love you, honey."

If you find yourself answering yes to any of these questions, you are, in fact, overindulging.

Children need to learn the value of a dollar—no matter how much that value has declined over the years. They need to understand what it means to sacrifice and go without the things they want, and what it means to give to others selflessly. To determine if your child is intoxicated by things, answer the following questions.

True or false:

- My child has more toys than she can use.
- My child doesn't say thank you.
- My child doesn't take care of her things.
- My child expects me to replace what he breaks.
- My child doesn't share.
- My child doesn't labor for what she has.
- My child never seems satisfied. The more we give him, the more he wants.

Whether your children are overindulged may depend on the age of your kids. For example, toddlers might not say thank you or share. Preteens might not take good care of their things, leaving their bikes in the rain and their CDs where they can get scratched.

Other factors are not necessarily bad in and of themselves. For instance, your kids may have more toys than they can use at once. But if you've found that more than half of these statements are true, and you've taken into account your child's age, she may be in fact too materialistic and overindulged.

How to Set Good Limits

You may have spent years doing everything from maxing out your credit card and throwing extravagant birthday parties to finishing your kids' math homework and writing their thank-you notes. Fortunately, it's never too late to make changes. Here are several practical ways you can help your kids learn to take responsibility for themselves and appreciate the things they've been given:

Try active listening.

Active listening is a good technique for parents who struggle with wanting to rescue their kids from tough situations. When parents use active listening, they let their children know they understand and appreciate their feelings and concerns, but they don't necessarily fix their kids' problems.

For example, your son walks into the kitchen, throws his backpack on the floor, and says, "I hate my science teacher. He's an idiot!"

He's obviously upset and frustrated. But he's also using words you don't like. You could get as irritated as he is and fire back, "Hey, don't talk that way around me!"

But doing that would just indicate to him that you care more about his manners than you do his feelings. It would also most likely backfire, since you would be barking at him while trying to teach him restraint.

Instead you could say, "You're obviously upset with him. What happened?"

"He's just a jerk!" your son maintains.

"Give me an example," you say. "Help me understand what he's done."

"He says we're not thinking or trying, and that we're the worst class he's had in ten years!"

Now you can respond to specifics. "It's probably a little rough to hear that from a teacher."

"But it's not true!" he says vehemently. "We do try. It's just that when he teaches, he makes no sense!"

You nod. "So he's difficult to understand and then blames you guys for not trying hard enough . . ."

As the conversation continues, your son begins to cool down, which gives you a chance to talk to him about name-calling and keeping his emotions in check. And by the end of your talk you find yourself agreeing with him—the teacher *is* a little difficult.

It's at this point that many overindulging parents go wrong, though. Once you understand the situation, you don't have to "fix" it. You've validated your son's feelings and talked to him about the name-calling. You don't have to march into your son's science class to confront the teacher, or do his science homework for him, or complain to the principal. It's a tough situation, but it's one your son can handle himself. If you complained to the principal or teacher, or did his homework, you'd be keeping him from learning, achieving, and gaining the confidence to deal with difficult people. By coaching your child through the process, you show *him* how to work through difficult situations, which will prepare him for life. Start by suggesting your child put things in context, asking himself: "Was I prepared for class?" "Was I preoccupied?" "Did anything unusual happen in class?" Then move on to coaching your child as to how he might address the situation with his teacher, such as "I want to be a good student. What can I do to better prepare for class?" "Are there study helps I can use?" "What would you suggest I do to improve my grades?" When teachers know a child honestly wants to do better, they'll almost always bend over backwards to help. Through this process, you are teaching your child to manage his own emotions and approach difficult situations with maturity, compassion, and integrity.

OFFER SUPPORT AND BRAINSTORMING.

Buying things for your kids or giving them freedoms isn't bad in and of itself. All kids are going to want toys and privileges. But instead of simply giving them what they want, try working with them to develop plans to achieve and earn those rewards.

For instance, your daughter says, "Mom, I want a laptop. Sarah and Kristy and Hannah all have one."

Normally, you'd be online right away, researching the best computer to get her. This time, however, you tell her, "Sure, you can get a laptop . . . But I'm not going to buy it for you."

"I'd have to save for ten years to get that much money!" she protests.

"What if I pay half," you suggest, "and you earn half?"

She shakes her head. "But I'm too young to get a job."

You brainstorm with her for a while, coming up with ways she can earn enough money, such as baby-sitting, washing cars, or walking dogs. You're impressed with her willingness to work, and you offer to give her some additional cash if she goes above and beyond her normal chores. She may not be happy about working to pay for half of the computer, but this way, she learns the value of money and appreciates the laptop when she finally earns it.

TRY PROBLEM SOLVING.

Many parents who overindulge haven't taught their child the fine art of negotiation and compromise. If Sean wants to go bowling, they go bowling—even if they've already been to the bowling alley twice that month.

But our authority as parents trumps our kids' will. Rather than drag the whole family to the bowling alley again, Sean's father should acknowledge that his son's feelings are important but then explain why they're going to the movies instead.

"I know you want to go bowling," he might say, "but we did that last time, so this time we're going someplace new."

An even better approach is to engage the child in collaborative problem solving. This way, both Sean and his dad can work together to find a solution they both agree on. His dad could explain, "I know you want to go bowling, but I'd rather go to the movies. So how can we work this out?" Often when parents include their kids in the decision—rather than letting them make the decision—their children will come up with a solution on their own. Sean might say, "Okay, but can we go bowling next time?" or "If we go to the movies, can I decide which one to see?"

The key to healthy problem solving is to respectfully acknowledge your child's concerns while asserting your own. Without teaching him these skills, he'll never learn how to come up with solutions that will satisfy both your needs.

STICK TO YOUR CONVICTIONS.

Some parents overindulge when they don't stick to their guns. "If you don't walk the dog," they might say, "you're not going to the movies later." But Andrew forgets, the dog remains unwalked, and when movie time comes, mom and dad feel sorry for Andrew and let him go anyway.

If you're not going to stand firm, don't make the rule. If you don't feel up to following through with consequences, don't threaten consequences. Your kids can read you, and they can tell by your tone of voice if you're serious. Check yourself before laying down the law. When you cave in, your children just lose respect for you and learn they are accountable to no one but themselves.

Make it a positive experience.

The best approach for getting your kids to take responsibility and help more around the house is to talk to them ahead of time so they can anticipate what they'll need to do. Then, as they complete their chores, praise them. If you can, work side by side with them so that you're bonding with them while you get things done. One parent told us, "Amazingly, Saturday morning is everyone's favorite time. We have a quick breakfast and then get started. The stereo goes on, we pull the blinds to let in the sunlight, and the whole family gets to work. We sweep, mop, vacuum, wash the windows and the dishes, clean out the refrigerator, scrub the bathrooms, and straighten the bedrooms. Everyone works hard for a couple of hours, and then we go have fun as a family. It's a great way to start a weekend!"

Tips for Celebrating Special Occasions

One of the most difficult times to set limits is during birthdays, holidays, or other special events. Unfortunately, most parents now equate exorbitant gift giving with love and fulfillment, and they pass that philosophy on to their kids. It is possible, however, to acknowledge these special times without overindulging.

When you try to set good limits, consider the maturity of

your children. Some gifts or privileges, such as owning a cell phone or attending boy-girl parties, may be appropriate for teenagers but not for young kids. We've listed some guidelines for making your holidays or other special events less focused on material things. If things still seem unclear, remember this general rule: overindulging is too much of a good thing, or a good thing given too soon.

LIMIT THE NUMBER OF PRESENTS.

It's the rare parent who hasn't seen his children go into a "feeding" frenzy Christmas morning as they dive into the pile of presents under the tree. Papers are ripped and fly everywhere as the kids thrash from gift to gift. It's usually too much for them to handle. Often what should be a happy Christmas morning turns to tears and acrimony as siblings fight about who got what toy and which child received the best stocking stuffers.

With this in mind, limit the gifts your children get to a reasonable number. To determine what is reasonable, follow your child's playing habits for thirty days after Christmas or a birthday. It will shock you how little meaning each gift has!

You also might want to control the emotional impact such an event has on your kids by opening half of the presents on Christmas Eve and the other half in the morning. By spacing out the gifts, children get the chance to recharge and even extend the anticipation, while parents get the opportunity to talk to their kids about gratitude and the purpose for giving and receiving at Christmas, Easter, and on birthdays and other special events.

GIVE GIFTS THE WHOLE FAMILY WILL ENJOY.

Consider gifts that grow and deepen your relationship with your kids, such as one-thousand-piece puzzles, board games, or video games where parents can compete. For example, the first gift my (Gary) family opens at Christmas is always a game we play together that morning. One year it was Nerf dartguns that sent us running through the living room, kitchen, and down the hall shooting foam darts at one another. The next year it was an air hockey game. Before we put the game away that night we had all become pretty good at slamming those plastic pucks around. None of these gifts cost a lot of money, but they all became the highlight of our Christmas. And when we tucked the kids in that night, we had some great stories to tell for many days afterward.

Other good gifts reinforce your children's dreams and ambitions, such as magic kits, baseball mitts, art supplies, or musical instruments. These presents can help teach your children, move them along the path to success, and remind them that you support their dreams.

TEACH THEM APPRECIATION.

Whether your children open all their gifts at once or spread them out over a few days, it's important that children realize they are receiving a gift, not an entitlement. Gifts require appreciation—appreciation for the gift itself and appreciation to the giver. Have your child first open and read the card. Then hand her the gift. Make sure your child opens the gift without tearing into it and makes a positive comment about the gift or even plays with it a bit before going on to the next one. If there are several people opening presents, take turns. Then, later, have your child write thank-you notes, explaining to the givers what she likes about the present and how much she appreciates the giver for sending it.

This will show your kids that the gift-giving process isn't just about them. Gifts include recipients, givers, the gifts themselves, and the thoughtfulness behind them. Children must be taught that no one is entitled to a gift, and that whether you receive one or many presents, you need to behave properly toward the gift and the giver.

DIALOGUE WITH THEM.

No matter how young your kids are, you can talk with them about the gift-giving process. You might encourage them to ask:

- Why has someone chosen to give me this specific gift?
- What did the giver have to give up or do to provide me with this gift?
- How can I show appreciation?

You, too, should reflect:

- Is this gift a bribe?
- Am I giving out of guilt?
- Am I infringing on teaching my child values by giving her this gift?
- Can we afford it?

GIVE BACK.

Children have a natural inclination to give. They spot a homeless man at a stoplight and they want to share their kid's meal. They see a television commercial that asks them to support a desperate child overseas and they run for their piggy bank.

The Bible says, "Give to the one who asks you, and do not turn away from the one who wants to borrow from you" (Matthew 5:42). Don't let this propensity fade. Harness it! Help them sponsor a needy kid. Take them to serve food at a local mission on Thanksgiving. Encourage your young children to give handmade gifts to family members at Christmas. Then praise them for giving and talk to them about what even a small gesture can mean to someone in need. It won't take long for them to realize it's much, much better to give than it is to get.

WALKING THE LINE

As parents, we must not only provide for our children but also teach them to take responsibility for their actions—a basic and important life lesson that's lost on many kids today. So instead of overindulging, try to:

- Reward hard work

- Encourage effort and reward

- Encourage healthy responsibility

- Encourage effort-driven activities like sports or music

Teaching your kids to become independent, to deal with the good and the bad things in life will help them grow and achieve their God-given purpose, the potential that God has envisioned for our lives!

As we watch our children mature and work through the inevitable successes and failures of life, we can remind them that Jesus is right by their side—to guide, to comfort, and to provide the wisdom and courage they need to stand strong.

chapter eight

Loving Without Overprotecting

For the LORD *your God moves about*
in your camp to protect you.

—Deuteronomy 23:14

𝒟on't play in the street." "Don't talk to strangers." "Bedtime is at nine o'clock." "First, you do your homework; then you can play." "No sleepovers this weekend. We need some family time." These are important parental controls—they're not overprotecting! So how do you know if you are overprotecting or simply being a caring, contentious parent?

According to the WordNet dictionary from Princeton University, the term *overprotection* has become so common among parents that to "overprotect" actually means to "care for like a mother."[1] But overprotection does not equal good parenting.

Dave came to us because he was having trouble with his seventeen-year-old daughter, Danielle. Dave's wife had died suddenly when Danielle was sixteen. Although Dave had never been particularly strict with Danielle before his wife's passing, now he was setting rules right and left. For instance, he wouldn't allow Danielle to get her driver's license, even though she was old enough.

"You're just not ready. You're not responsible enough," he would say.

"But why not?" Danielle protested. "I'm the only one in my class that doesn't have a driver's license. The only one!"

"Don't argue with me!" Dave always told her. "Your room isn't picked up! How can I trust you with a car when you can't even keep your room clean?"

The same reasoning applied to dating, hanging out with friends, and even going on school-sponsored fieldtrips—Danielle just wasn't "responsible enough," and David was rarely convinced the arrangements were safe anyway. Dave was trying to physically protect both of them: Danielle from basic, teenage activities, and himself from losing his daughter like he lost his wife.

Other parents try to protect their kids socially. One mother told us, "The neighborhood kids can be so cruel! Jeffrey seems to do fine, but watching him be subjected to teasing is more than I can handle. So I make up an excuse to keep him inside, telling him, 'You need to help me with the laundry.'"

She did this nearly all summer to protect Jeffrey from the neighborhood teasing—more or less normal kid behavior. Instead of coaching her son to be confident and assertive, teaching him to face adversity and then overcome it, she hindered his emotional and social development.

It would have been more beneficial to Jeffrey if his mom had helped him learn how to deal with the teasing. A good way to do this is to talk with your child about a third person. It is not nearly as threatening to help another person work through their problems as to address our own. Children feel the same way. You might start with questions such as, "Have you ever seen someone get teased? What should that person do? What could we do to make that person feel important?" At this point remind your child he is loved. Help him focus on his strengths. Only then should you talk with your child about the teasing he is experiencing.

When parents overprotect, it is because they don't want their child to experience normal suffering. But overprotecting is more harmful than many parents realize, and can be just as destructive to a child's development as many forms of abuse.[2]

Two Kinds of Pain

"Life is difficult," wrote Scott Peck in his 1978 classic *The Road Less Traveled*,[3] for difficulty is a part of even the best-lived lives. We all know our kids will experience difficulty. And it's normal for us—it's a natural, God-given instinct—to want to shield them from that pain. But sometimes protecting our loved ones from pain is not loving at all. Suffering is always uncomfortable, but it isn't always bad. In fact, sometimes it's necessary for emotional and spiritual health.

It has been said that the cause of all unnecessary, self-defeating pain is the avoidance of legitimate pain.[4] Legitimate pain is pain we must work through in order to achieve a greater good or a higher purpose. For instance, athletes must train through physical pain, battling muscle aches, broken bones, bruises, and the anguish of defeat if they want to achieve victory. Similarly, high school students who want to get into prestigious colleges may have to study when their friends are out having fun. We can safely say this: if it's important, if it truly matters, if your life will be better with it than without it, getting it will involve pain or sacrifice.

Ironically, if we try to avoid necessary pain, we will be ravaged by self-defeating pain.[5] Athletes who avoid the pain of hard training end up defeated or injured when they attempt a feat they are not properly trained for. College students who squander their freshman year by partying can end up on academic probation.

Spiritual growth requires the same discipline. Paul explained, "Therefore I do not run like a man running aimlessly; I do not fight like a man beating the air. No, I beat my body and make it my slave so that after I have preached to others, I myself will not be disqualified for the prize" (1 Corinthians 9:26–27).

The Bible commands Christians to welcome the difficulties we will inevitably face when we undergo spiritual training. Paul, who dealt with beatings, incarceration, persecution, and his own struggle with sin, wrote, "We also rejoice in our sufferings, because we know that suffering produces perseverance; perseverance, character; and character, hope" (Romans 5:3–4).

When we learn how to persevere or endure pain such as disappointment, anxiety, boredom, and sacrifice, we develop character. We become optimistic and disciplined. We begin to wait on God. Through such suffering, we also learn to consider the needs of others.

The challenge is to find the balance. Of course we want to protect our children from unnecessary pain! However, we need to know our kids well enough to discern when they aren't up to the challenge and when they have the strength to work things out. This means letting them face life experiences and people that will stretch them. And while they're learning and developing, dusting them off and getting them back in the race.

Healthy Protecting from Birth to Adulthood

When infants fill their lungs with air for the first time, they are dependent upon their parents for everything—food, warmth, and most importantly, love. Parents quickly learn when their children are hungry, tired, wet, sick, cold, and need changing, and they meet those needs night and day.

When babies are only a few months old, though, parents begin to give them a little responsibility. They learn to hold a bottle and to use silverware to feed themselves. At around two or three, children are toilet-trained, and a little later they take on the responsibility of bathing themselves. When parenting is successful, children will slowly learn to control their behavior and emotions, becoming increasingly responsible and independent. In doing so they relinquish their parents from a life of caregiving and total servitude.

For this process to work, parents must balance helping and protecting their children with maintaining enough distance to allow their kids some freedom and responsibility. Further, parents must always be "on call" and ready to intervene when necessary. This is a difficult task. No parent gets the protection-freedom balance right 100 percent of the time. Sometimes we turn around to find our children in danger. But more often we're too cautious; we overprotect when we should let them venture out and make some of their own choices—even if they get hurt a little.

God has built into our genetic code a desire for growth and independence. At the same time, we also have a natural desire to remain safe and close to our secure bases. These two desires often come into conflict, especially for parents. One parent said about her teenage daughter, "It's like watching your child learn how to swing on a trapeze at a circus; you watch her let go of one handle and close your eyes, praying she grasps the next one safely . . ."

Don't misunderstand; we aren't advocating that you let your children do anything you believe is immoral, excessively harmful, or risky. However, we are suggesting that you let your kids try out for football, or the high school play, or submit their writings for publication, even when there's a good chance they'll be rejected—and hurt.

Kids are remarkably resilient. And many times things turn out just fine, without our meddling. Even if Jonah doesn't make varsity football this year, he'll probably get on the junior varsity team. And who knows, Julie could get the lead in the play!

Still, in today's world, it's helpful to have some guidelines to determine what's healthy protecting. Though the amount of protection parents need to provide their children differs depending on the child's age, maturity, temperament, and environment, there are ways to determine whether the protection you're providing fits within a healthy range.

AGES 0–3

It's almost impossible to give a baby too much love and attention. As children form their personalities and core beliefs about themselves, the world, and their place in it, they look to their parents for answers. They wonder, *Is the world safe? Can I trust people?* To find out, they listen—and watch. Do their parents say there's nothing to worry about, but then keep a gun in the closet for protection? Do they say not to judge people, but then cross the street to avoid the man with piercings and tattoos?

Kids see everything. And their parents' attitudes, prejudices, and assorted elements of wisdom make up the lens through which they develop a worldview. If mom and dad generally keep promises, they believe that it's likely others will too. If they break promises, keep them waiting in the rain, put them in difficult or dangerous situations, or are emotionally unavailable, children reason that others will probably do the same. So if their parents proclaim that "the world is dangerous" by overprotecting, why should kids believe differently?

It's important for us to censor our young kids' environment—for example, to install childproof locks on cupboards and plastic plugs over electrical outlets—and to teach them how to protect themselves. It's crucial that we explain, "Don't touch a hot stove!" "Don't hit!" and "Don't talk to strangers!" But even in these early, impressionable years, there are freedoms we can provide them to help them gain healthy independence.

Tips for Balanced Protecting (Ages 0-3)

Freedoms	Restrictions
1. Allow your child to crawl or walk outside the house, even if there is some risk of minor bumps and bruises.	1. Protect him from physically harmful items (cleaning products, electrical outlets, stairs, etc).
2. Don't be too hypersensitive about what your child puts in her mouth. Exposure to germs helps strengthen the immune system and build antibodies.	2. Correct her when it's likely she will hurt herself or others. For example, "Let go of the cat's tail!" or "Don't eat that, honey. That fell in the street."
3. When he's three years old, allow your child some independence during playtime. For instance, let him use the playground sandbox by himself.	3. Encourage him to explore but be available whenever he starts feeling insecure. Pay particular attention to transitions, sudden shifts in schedules, illnesses, and when he is hungry or sleepy. These are times he will need extra help getting calm and dealing with frustration.
4. Offer your child some selection of activities and foods.	4. Set her sleep schedule and basic menu.
5. Let your child express strong emotions.	5. Help him calm down when he gets upset. Display your morals. For instance you might say, "It's okay to be angry, but it's not okay to hit your brother."

Ages 4–7

At about age four, children become more social as they seek out relationships with people other than their mom and dad. By this time, they have had their first experiences playing with their neighborhood, preschool, or kindergarten friends. This smalltime venturing out is for many parents the first time they come eyeball to eyeball with the fact they're not able to completely control and censor their child's environment. From the moment Mom puts Charlie on the bus, she relinquishes all control and must trust the bus driver to keep her son safe—and then trust the teachers and administrators to do the same until that bus driver brings Charlie home.

Some parents quickly adapt and even begin to enjoy their freedom. Others find this separation terrifying. They become nuisances to the bus driver: "I don't want Zoe crossing the street there." And the bane of schoolteachers: "Are you sure the desk won't collapse? Will you tell her to wear her jacket at recess?" They harass the cafeteria workers: "Are those fresh carrots? How much fat is in that gravy?" And they monitor the P.E. staff: "I don't want my child on those monkey bars. And Zoe better not get overheated if you have her run laps. She's a delicate little girl."

Although moms and dads have the best intentions, such behavior can interfere greatly with their children's development.[6] Overprotection can rob your kids of the opportunity to problem solve and manage their behavior. Ironically, this can leave them feeling vulnerable and fragile, the opposite of what overprotective parents intend to instill.

Tips for Balanced Protecting (Ages 4–7)

Freedoms	Restrictions
1. Allow your child to decorate his bedroom (within reason).	1. Make sure he keeps his room clean.
2. Allow her to choose what clothes she'll wear from her closet.	2. Moderate the clothes she chooses and purchase appropriate clothing for her.
3. If you live in a generally safe area, let him play outside with friends.	3. Restrict how far he can venture from home.
4. Let your child participate in extracurricular activities, such as joining a Brownie or Cub Scout troop.	4. Volunteer to chaperone fieldtrips.
5. Allow her to attend play dates away from your home.	5. Host some play dates in your home.

Ages 8–14

As kids become more capable and begin to explore their world, they desire more independence. "Mom," they might initially ask, "can I ride my bike *all the way* to the end of the street?" "Dad, can I play in the woods by the reservoir?" Growing children want to make choices that reflect their dreams, interests—and sense of invincibility. Even as young kids, they want to set their own bedtime, choose what food they eat, and play with the attack dog next door.

When kids elbow their way into adolescence, they want to differentiate themselves from their parents with their tastes and preferences. For instance, Kate is the only one in her family who likes mushrooms. Nate's favorite music is hip-hop—much to his parents' dismay. And Gabby can't stand the bell-bottoms in her mom's closet. This process, in which kids become more influenced by the peers and less by their parents, is what famous psychologist Eric Erikson called "individuation."[7]

At this point, both parents and kids begin to experience a certain amount of separation anxiety. Kids start looking to their friends as their security and are less inclined to talk with their parents about their concerns. This can be a tremendously challenging time for overprotective parents. After all, they can hardly trust their child with other adults, let alone other teenagers.

At the same time that kids are on a quest to discover their own identity, they are also going through extreme hormone changes. The comedian J. Allen speculated, "The Bible doesn't say how old Satan was when he disputed with God and fell from grace, but I'm guessing he was about thirteen."[8] But take heart: if you have a strong relationship with your children going into adolescence, your kids will usually accept your rules and guidance. Young teens look to their peers for their taste in music, clothes, and movies, but they are still much more influenced by their parents when it comes to larger issues like drinking, drugs, religion, and morals.[9] The key is to remain involved but not overcontrolling or overprotective. If you and your child are constantly locked in a power struggle, your influence will be greatly weakened.

Of course, with this freedom comes plenty of angst. Remember trying to find a date for the freshman dance, not making the cheerleading squad, losing the election for eighth-grade president, or being called a loser because you chose to serve Christ? These are all pains your adolescents will need to experience. Watching your kids go through this is not easy, but it is necessary. The best advice we can give to parents is that there is "a time to embrace and a time to refrain" (Ecclesiastes 3:5). At thirteen, parents need to at least loosen their grip.

You may have to ask yourself some tough questions as to why your child's budding independence is so threatening to you. One mother-daughter pair we worked with was enthroned in battles about friends and phone time. The daughter, Andrea, wanted to talk with her friends on the phone, which included both girls and guys. Her mother, Robin, was obsessed with the idea that her daughter, who was more physically developed than most thirteen-year-olds, was having "deviant" conversations about sex and drugs.

"It worries me," Robin told us. "You know how people are these days. They're just looking for an opportunity to take advantage of a girl like her. You just can't be too safe."

There was no reason to think her daughter was into any of this. She was a great kid who was living a great life. Predictably, Andrea was angry. "It's like my mom wants me to keep a phone log about who I talk to, when I talk, and what we talk about," she said. "It makes me mad because I don't get into trouble but I'm treated like I'm a troublemaker."

As Andrea got more angry, Robin got more protective. Gently, we challenged Robin's view of the world and helped her explore some tough questions about her upbringing. As a young girl, Robin had been sexually abused by family friends. Gradually, as she was able to talk about this experience, she became more aware of how it influenced her relationship with her daughter. It took time, but as she learned to trust Andrea and give her appropriate independence, Robin began to heal from her own past—to grieve the loss of her innocence and revise her view of the world.

TIPS FOR BALANCED PROTECTING (AGES 8–14)

FREEDOMS	RESTRICTIONS
1. Allow your child more social freedom.	1. Establish a curfew.
2. Let him select television programs and movies.	2. Censor offensive and obscene material. Talk to him about what he's viewing.
3. Let your child choose her own hobbies.	3. Set appropriate limits to the amount of time your child spends in these activities.
4. Let him choose his friends.	4. Talk to him about the things you like and dislike about his friends' behavior and values— not about them as people.
5. Let your child select what clothes to buy.	5. Make sure her selections are responsible and appropriate.
6. Let her talk on the phone.	6. Monitor her computer use and install parental controls to protect her from inappropriate content.
7. Make your home interesting and allow your teen to have friends spend the night. Get to know his friends without doing a "background check." Learn how to talk with teenagers.	7. If your child goes to a friend's house to spend the day or night, check in with his friend's parents to ensure they'll be appropriately monitoring the kids' activities.

AGES 14–17

All parents worry about peer pressure when their child hits the teen years. But even if they don't show it, teens continue to look to their parents for guidance throughout adolescence. As we noted earlier, research repeatedly proves that pop culture and peers get the nod when it comes to music, clothes, and fun, but parents are by far the strongest influence in big issues such as sex, drugs, faith, and their place in the world. Teens who don't smoke, drink, or take drugs say it was their parents who influenced them to stay clean. They respect their parents' clearly stated positions. They might temporarily rebel, but children are likely to return to those good early teachings of their parents. The Bible confirms this, saying, "How can a young man keep his way pure? By living according to your word" (Psalm 119:9 NIV).

Remember, your task is not to protect your kids at all costs—it is to help them learn to think for and protect themselves! Instead of keeping your child from hanging out with her friends because you're afraid that she'll experiment with drugs, ask questions like, "What do you think about drinking?" and "How would you respond if someone pressured you to smoke or do drugs?"

Then instead of focusing on just what she thinks, encourage her to explain why. If she says, "Well, I wouldn't take the cigarette," ask her why. That way she'll be doing more than just reciting a line—she'll be thinking things through. Of course, many teens will resist, mumbling, "I don't know, just because . . ." When she dodges the question, gently ask her to explain herself before you allow her to go out with her friends.

Doing this will not only strengthen her confidence and

convictions, it will also help her learn to think for herself. For example, if your daughter says she wants to spend the night with Britney, you might reply, "That sounds like a possibility—I know you and Britney are good friends. What do you like about spending time with her?" You can also use this method to help her learn responsibility. You could say, "You've still got a ton of work to do on that English paper. How are you going to finish that if you're spending the night at Britney's?" Of course, your daughter won't like being questioned, especially if she has trouble expressing herself verbally, but it will help her learn to be responsible even as she's embracing her newfound freedom.

Part of healthy parenting is teaching your children to express themselves and stand up for what they believe. But how do you give them the confidence to do that—especially during the teen years? One way is to nurture their strengths. Help your child identify what he's good at, and then find ways to encourage him to express his strengths, whether it's through writing, sports, computers, music, or serving others. Compliments also go a long way. "You know," you could say, "when Braden sings, I hear angels. And those comic books he does are hysterical! I'm so proud of my son." Every chance you get, tell your friends and relatives. And make sure he hears you. Your son might act embarrassed when you boast about him, but inside he's beaming with joy.

Of course, teenagers are bound to miss the mark from time to time. Even the most well-behaved kids will rebel and test the boundaries. When this happens, your first inclination will be to overprotect to make sure your child never gets hurt again. But there are some lessons that just can't be learned without pain. Sometimes happiness hurts! Rather than overprotect, take the opportunity to teach your child to repent, pray, and reconsider his actions. In doing this, you'll be helping him take responsibility for his mistakes, aiding in his personal and spiritual growth.

TIPS FOR BALANCED PROTECTING (AGES 14–17)

FREEDOMS	RESTRICTIONS
1. Allow your teen to apply for her license.	1. Make sure she drives responsibly.
2. Let him decide when to complete his homework.	2. Make sure he maintains adequate grades.
3. Allow her to choose a college to attend.	3. Set parameters for things it is important to look for in a university.
4. Let your child choose his level of participation in church activities.	4. Provide him with spiritual guidance. Make attending church on Sunday mornings a family rule.
5. Let your teen participate in normal social activities.	5. Make sure she is not unduly exposed to drugs and alcohol, and is in a safe, supervised environment.

AGES 18 AND UP

When children turn eighteen, they become legal adults, and parents enter what we call the "launching phase," where they send their young ones into the world to be independent and self-reliant adults. At this stage, it's important for parents to let go and trust God that their child is properly equipped to make good decisions based on the morals and values he learned growing up. This is an important biblical concept. Jesus says, "For this reason a man will leave his father and mother and be united to his wife" (Matthew 19:5). He doesn't say, "Grown-up kids should stay with their parents and depend on them for their every material and emotional need."

Of course when you launch your child into adulthood, you aren't ending the relationship; you're beginning a new phase. Now that your "child" is an adult, you need to give him the same respect you would any other adult. You can still be involved in his life, but you're no longer his disciplinarian and guardian; you're more like his mentor—a trusted counselor or guide.

Although for many parents this is a joyous time, a time when marital and life satisfaction skyrockets, parents who overprotect tend to find it frightening. They often hold on tightly to their children, fearing their kids will make poor choices or that they'll be left behind as their children enter adulthood. But clinging to them will only foster resentment and rebellion. Kids must be allowed to move on.

Ken, a single father, came to us looking for help with his rebellious nineteen-year-old son, Mike. Ken had heard that his son was getting drunk at local bars. "Not only that," Ken told us, "but Mike also moved in with his friends—a place with no rules, where his girlfriend can spend the night!"

"It's probably very difficult to watch your son make those choices," we acknowledged. "But Mike's an adult now, Ken. He has his own free will. It may be some time before he learns to use that freedom responsibly.

"Don't give up," we hastened. "The best approach is for you to remain faithful to Jesus. Instead of worrying, try to lift up your child to the Lord in prayer. This is where your faith becomes reality, as you trust God to work in Mike's heart and life. While you do this, be available to Mike when he returns to you for guidance. Most likely, he will turn to you for help, though it may not be until his world begins to crumble."

We also encouraged Ken to write his son a letter. After a lot of thought, Ken wrote:

Dear Mike,

I wanted to write you this short letter to tell you some things I feel very strongly about. First, I want you to know that I will always be your father. I will be here for you—for guidance, support, and love—for as long as I am alive. However, I also understand that you are now an adult. You are a man, and I have no authority over you or anything you do. As an adult, you are responsible for your own choices, whether they bring failure or success. I truly pray that you will find happiness and success.

I've done the best I know how to raise you well and teach you what I believe are important life lessons. As you know, I do not approve of all your recent decisions. But they are your choices, not mine, and I respect that. Even when I do not approve of your decisions, I will still love you. And I will always be here for you when you need me.

Your loving father,

Ken

This message is critical. Whether you discuss this in person or by letter, it is important that you release your child, letting him know that he is now a full-fledged adult who has hopefully learned to bear both the freedoms and responsibilities of life with integrity and Christian character.

If your child, like Ken's, is headed down the wrong path, don't lose hope. Scripture tells the famous story of the prodigal son, who squandered his inheritance, living a life that we are led to believe included prostitutes, drugs, and other idolatry (Luke 15:11–32). This desperate father knew his son was doomed to bad choices and understood he was powerless to change him. Amazingly, he remained vigilant, available, and loving. When his son returned, asking forgiveness, the father put a ring on his son's finger, placed a robe over his shoulders, and threw a party.

Like the prodigal son, some adult children may abandon their parents' values when they leave home. Others—especially kids who have been overprotected—may resist leaving home at all. These adults, often in their late twenties or early thirties, prefer to stay living rent-free with their parents. If your adult-child won't leave home, you must lovingly get her on track, requiring her to find her own apartment and a job to pay her own bills. You may feel as if you're "kicking her out," but in reality, you're helping her take responsibility for her own life.

When you have successfully guided—not overprotected—your child toward adulthood, your relationship with her will slowly begin to shift. The apostle Paul instructed children, "Children or grandchildren, these should learn first of all to put their religion into practice by caring for their own family and so repaying their parents and grandparents, for this is pleasing to God" (1 Timothy 5:4). As the Bible indicates, our relationship with our kids is cyclical—as they become adults, they are supposed to care for and protect us.

Providing Godly Support and Help to Your Now-Adult Child

- Don't condone the behavior. Your past sin does not excuse your child's sin.

- Confront the behavior in love.

- Respect her autonomy and rights. She is an adult now.

- Pray.

- If things are out of control (if there is drug use, violence, depression, debilitating anxiety, or potential suicide), consider professional intervention.

INTO GOD'S PERFECT CARE

Author and child-care expert Grace Ketterman says, "Releasing young people into today's world is a panicky process. This process can be made more reassuring when parents remember that they are transferring them from the shelter of their parental wings to the perfect care of the heavenly Father."[10]

It is our task as parents to build up our children in the ways of the Lord. That includes infusing our kids with independence and a Christlike mind-set, giving them the ability to eventually have dominion over their own lives. It is a frightening and often heart-wrenching process, but it is the final call of good parenting.

chapter nine

Loving Without Overcontrolling

The vast majority of our children are not dazzlingly brilliant, extremely witty, highly coordinated, tremendously talented, or universally popular! They are just ordinary kids with oversized needs to be loved and accepted as they are.[1]

Dr. James Dobson

*Y*ou got a C in Spanish? I can't believe you, Christopher! Are you trying to embarrass us?" Bill screamed. "No son of mine is going to get anything less than an A, do you understand? You'll never amount to anything if you continue to get Cs. You *will* raise this grade, and you *will* stay after school every day until this grade is an A. Until then, you're grounded!"

Every day we see parents like Bill who are pushing their kids to the max, pressuring them to be the best on the cheerleading squad, the smartest in the classroom, and the most talented in the school play. They shuttle their children to try-outs, practices, and SAT prep courses, correcting and critiquing them all the way. These kids have little time for relaxation or fun. They quickly learn that they are valued for what they can achieve, instead of who they are.

This kind of pushing and overcontrolling has become so prevalent that reams of newsprint and hours of television have been devoted to the topic. Several years ago, fifty thousand parents participating in a national survey were asked to list the qualities they most wanted in their children. Intelligence placed highest, along with concern about giving children stimulation, enrichment, and a head start, while values such as honesty, trust, or love did not even make the list.[2] It's a sad commentary on the state of parenting today, but it's not surprising.

When I (Tim) was in the high-pressure dynamic of graduate school, a wise instructor had to continually reiterate to her very driven class, "Failing to get an A on an exam is not failing in life." Unfortunately, overcontrolled kids don't have the discernment and maturity to understand that—especially if their parents have only given them conditional love and affection.

These parents don't gently guide their kids through life. They bark commands and issue criticism at their children at every step, expecting their kids to achieve perfection. Yet instead of helping their kids become "the best," most often these parents push them to toxic levels of insecurity. When children are judged on what they produce, their self-esteem suffers tremendously. Overcontrolled kids feel inadequate when they don't set the academic curve or hit every baseball out of the park. They fall into what we call the performance trap, defining success as being the best instead of doing your best.

They also fall into the approval trap, placing too much value on the opinions of others. These kids feel inadequate and unworthy if people don't like them. As young kids, they worry about their parents' approval, and as teens, they become incredibly susceptible to unhealthy peer pressure. Often, they'll compromise their beliefs and values just to ensure that their friends like them.

How Do You Measure Up?

You will . . . stand up straight. You will . . . bring up those grades. You will . . . be home by 7 o'clock. You will . . . go to college. You will . . . enjoy yourself. You will . . . not see that boy/girl anymore.

Sound familiar? If you tend to overcontrol, you've probably said most of these things to your kids—sometimes in the space of a few hours!

Most overcontrolling parents we meet believe with all their heart they are doing the right thing by being so "involved." Often, they've grown up in very strict, harsh, and overcontrolled environments themselves. Some are perfectionists and put a lot of pressure on themselves, naturally transferring that pressure to their children. They live vicariously through their kids' successes and failures. Though they appear to have it all together, these parents often have deep-seated feelings of inadequacy. Their insecurities are usually unapparent when their kids are young and need them for so many things, such as feeding, bathing, diaper changes, protection, and love. But as their infants blossom into toddlers, school-age kids, and then teenagers, they become less needed. And instead of feeling grateful and accomplished, these parents feel useless. *My children don't need me*, they tell themselves. *I'm not good for anything.*

As a result, overcontrolling parents often want to make their children dependent upon them forever, even into adulthood. They try to make important decisions for their kids, choosing their career, pastimes, friendships, lifestyle, and religious beliefs, and they do that—either knowingly or unknowingly—by making their children feel inadequate. "You're doing that wrong," they might say. "Without my help, you wouldn't be able to survive on your own." Or, "You said *what?* You really should have talked to me before you interviewed for that job."

They may say they want their kids to have their own dreams and desires, but in reality, overcontrolling parents usually want their children to be more successful clones of themselves. If dad went to law school, then so should Jaden—but he better be at the top of his class. If mom worked on the student paper, then so should Stephanie—but she better be editor-in-chief! These parents see their child's differences not as part of their child's unique nature, but as a parenting failure.

They also injure their kids with what they think is love. It's easy for them to think they're helping Josh by forcing him to join the football team. *He'll bulk up and be more confident*, they tell themselves, *and he might get a scholarship out of it.* But what does Josh think? *My parents don't care about the fact that I hate football. I guess I'm only good enough for them if I'm on the team.*

As we've said before, it's our job as parents to provide

instruction and guidance for our kids. But what's the difference between guidance and overcontrol? How do you know if you're being a caring parent or you're really just too invested? Take a moment to think about the last few conversations you've had with your kids before asking yourself these questions:

Five Questions to Identify Overcontrol

- Does my child have trouble expressing his values, preferences, or uniqueness?

- Do I have a selfish motive for raising a strong and healthy kid?

- Am I upsetting, hurting, or discouraging my child?

- Do I have biblical support for the ways I control my child?

- Does my controlling prevent my child from completing any developmental tasks, such as building self-confidence, empathy, or problem-solving skills?

If you find yourself answering yes to any of these questions, you may have a problem with overcontrol. If so, don't be discouraged! We know that many parents who overcontrol do so out of good intentions and concerns—not because they don't love their kids.

How to Give Balanced Control

The good news is that you can stop the cycle. It may be a challenge, but you can begin to balance control with grace and love. One of the first ways to do this is to look to Scripture for guidance.

The Bible teaches that our value is not dependent on the grades we earn, the languages we speak, the friends we have, or the money we make. We are all created in the image and spirit of God (see Genesis 1:27). Our worth is based on who we are, not what we do. God gives us the grace to make mistakes. The Bible says, "But now a righteousness from God, apart from law, has been made known, to which the Law and the Prophets testify. This righteousness from God comes through faith in Jesus Christ to all who believe . . . All have sinned and fall short of the glory of God, and are justified freely by his grace through the redemption that came by Christ Jesus" (Romans 3:21–24). If God gives us, His children, this kind of grace, shouldn't we as earthly parents impart such grace to our kids?

Our heavenly Father provides the perfect example of balanced control. He doesn't constantly judge or criticize. In fact, He cherishes us—every fiber of our being. King David wrote in a song to God, "For you created my inmost being; you knit me together in my mother's womb. I praise you because I am fearfully and wonderfully made; your works are wonderful, I know that full well" (Psalm 139:13–14). God loves us no matter what. We may disappoint Him, but our actions won't change His love for us. He stands by our side, guiding us through life. He cheers us on when we succeed, comforts us when we fail, and waits patiently for us to return to Him when we lose our way.

Here are a few practical ways that you, following God's model of perfect control, can begin to lovingly let go:

LET THEM EXPRESS THEIR OPINIONS AND TASTES.

Kids are going to have likes and dislikes that differ from yours. Sometimes these differences are minor. "I love cats, but my parents don't—they're allergic," a young girl once said to us. And sometimes they're more drastic. "His mother and I are Republicans, but our son is as left as a Christian can be!" one father said jovially. Whatever your differences are, there's no healthy way to make your children prefer what you prefer or believe what you believe. As parents, we are to teach our kids good morals and biblical principles, and then with their opinions set them free.

If your child disagrees with you, don't jump to the conclusion that he's a moral reprobate and needs to be intimidated into changing his mind. For example, after tackling the subject in a high school debate, your sixteen-year-old son decides he is an avid proponent of legalizing drugs. You could say, "What?! I can't believe you think that! Do you *know* what the Bible says about substance abuse? Wait . . . are you on drugs? You're not leaving this house for the rest of the school year, young man!" If you do, we guarantee he'll become even more entrenched in his beliefs. Instead, ask with curiosity and interest why he believes what he does. "Why do you think that's the right solution?" you might respond. Ask him to explain how his worldview would affect others, and how it might work out for him in the future.

Allowing your kids to have their own opinions doesn't mean you're relinquishing your authority. If your daughter is arguing passionately that curfews are pointless, you don't have to give in. You can simply say, "I know you think that all sixteen-year-olds should be able to stay out as long as they like, but our rule is that you're home by 11:00 p.m. on the weekends."

EXAMINE YOUR MOTIVES.

Some parents look at their kids as an investment. They want their children to succeed because they want the payout! Sometimes the expectations are financial: *she's going to become a doctor and move her father and I into a mansion!* But more often they're social: *when he gets into Princeton, that'll show everyone.*

Most kids will rebel against their parents to escape these suffocating expectations. Even if they don't, however, their self-esteem will be contingent on how they will one day be able to reimburse their parents. We as parents should want our kids to succeed, to have a good life. But our children are not the "ultimate project" or investment.

LET YOUR CHILD COMPLETE HIS OR HER OWN DEVELOPMENTAL TASKS.

Developmental tasks are those milestones that kids must reach in their journey between infancy and adulthood: from first steps to first days at school, first slumber parties to first dates, from their first time behind the wheel to their first semester at college, it's important for kids to reach these milestones by their own effort. It may be tempting to hover and provide constant advice, but it won't help them in the long run.

This doesn't mean that you can't be there to provide emotional first aid for their occasional bumps and bruises. In fact, it's essential that you do this! But you need to begin to let go and let them move forward.

UNDERSTANDING AND ACCEPTING YOUR KIDS

As we've stated, many parents who overcontrol not only try to monitor their kids' actions—they want to change their children's personalities, the essence of who they are! One such parent, George, came to see us one week with his teenage son, Caleb. For several years, George, a high-powered real-estate broker, had been coaching Caleb's football team. At first, Caleb seemed to like that his dad was so involved in his life, but as time went on, he began to withdraw from George more and more.

"He just tunes me out," said George, pointing to his sullen son. "When I give football pep-talks, all the other kids get pumped up and are ready to go out there and chew up the field. But Caleb just stares at me like he's annoyed. It doesn't matter what I do. I can yell, I can critique, I can get in his face, but I can't get any emotion out of him."

Caleb would also tune him out in the mornings. "I come in and open the blinds at 7:00 a.m. when he's not in school,"

George explained. "I don't want to raise a lazy boy. In this house, we expect our kids to get moving and get things done! Plus, mornings are the best time of the day. Everybody knows that. But when I throw open his door, Caleb just scowls at me."

It didn't take us long to get to the bottom of the problem. Unlike his excitable and overbearing dad, Caleb was a somewhat awkward, laid-back young man.

"What do you do for fun, Caleb?" we asked, turning the conversation from his dad.

"Well . . ." Caleb said in a soft-spoken voice. "I really like computers. And I like to draw and go mountain biking up in the hills by our house."

"So you like activities that allow you to think and be by yourself?"

Caleb nodded.

"What about music?" we queried. "Would you rather listen to loud music or quiet music?"

"Loud music gives me a headache."

"Caleb," we asked him quietly, "do you like football?"

"Of course he likes football!" George interjected. "Caleb loves football!"

We turned to George. "Let's give Caleb a chance to answer."

Caleb studied his hands for several minutes and glanced over at his dad.

"It's okay," we told the boy. "There's no wrong answer."

"I guess I like football. I like practice. I like the exercise part—stretching and running and some of the drills," he began slowly. "But . . . uh . . . I don't really like all the yelling, and I hate game day because of all the chaos. I like practicing at night when the field is empty."

Like many children who are overcontrolled, Caleb didn't know exactly what he liked and what he didn't like. His type-A dad had always answered and made those decisions for him! George loved Caleb, but he didn't understand him. Instead of letting his son be the shy, laid-back kid God designed him to be, George had been trying to mold Caleb after himself: a high-energy, social football star. It took several counseling sessions, but eventually we helped George better understand—and accept—his son's personality and preferences.

Parents like George who overcontrol often try to change their child's inborn, God-given character traits. They will push their child, trying to jostle him "out of his box," because, after all, "it's for his own good." Of course, what they're really saying to their child is, "You are not acceptable how you are. You need to be more like me!"

Research shows that we all have nine inborn characteristics that appear at birth and remain with us through adulthood. When parents and their kids match up in temperament, getting along is easy. But when those character qualities differ between parents and children—particularly when mom or dad is overcontrolling—conflict often results.

Let's take a look at the nine inborn characteristics:

ADAPTABILITY

Some people enjoy change. They restyle their hair, rearrange furniture, and frequently change their e-mail address. Others find it stressful. Once they have things the way they want, they'll do anything to keep it that way.

Parents can determine their kids' adaptability very early in life by seeing what happens when they change their brand of diapers or baby food, or what happens when their baby is put to bed or woken up at an irregular time. Does he take it in stride, or does he become fussy, anxious, and upset? If your child was the kind of baby who couldn't be schlepped around from place to place or taken off his schedule, chances are he's still that way—and as much as you might try, you won't be able to change him.

ACTIVITY LEVEL

Some mothers claim that even before birth they can determine their child's activity level. How often the baby kicks, flips, and reacts in the womb can predict whether she'll be active or more laid back.

When parent and child have the same activity level, things are simple. When activity levels differ, though, watch out. What happens when you want to go on a five-mile hike and your daughter wants to watch TV? Or your son wants to play tennis and you'd rather sit, chat, and drink coffee together? One mother, feeling rejected by her daughter, told us, "I try to connect with Lauren. Several times a day, I'll say, 'Lauren, come sit next to Mommy, and I'll read this story to you.' But it takes me twenty minutes just to get her to sit down, and then three minutes later she's off running around the room again!" Instead of trying to make your child keep the same activity level you do, take some time to reflect on what she needs, and if possible, follow her lead.

DISTRACTIBILITY

Usually when people think about distractibility, they picture a focused parent with a fidgety child. We often see the opposite, though—like the little girl who can play contentedly with her dolls for hours, and the mom who can't focus for ten minutes and is constantly in her daughter's business. "Come on, let's go to the mall," her mother might say. "You need to get out anyway. I'll buy you something. How does a chocolate sundae sound?"

INTENSITY

Some intense parents, especially those who overcontrol, have no idea what to do with mellow, shy children. Other, more laid-back parents can be absolutely overwhelmed by their hyper, intense kids. Remember the cartoon "Dennis the Menace"? This high-strung, inquisitive little boy was the perfect foil to his low-key neighbor friend Mr. Wilson. "Mr. Wilson!" Dennis would say. "What are you doing, Mr. Wilson? Why are you doing that, Mr. Wilson? Want to go fishing, Mr. Wilson? Want to see my new baseball, Mr. Wilson? Look Mr. Wilson!" Mr. Wilson responded by ignoring Dennis and sometimes even blowing up at him. But his wife, Mrs. Wilson, understood that Dennis had the intensity of a raging bull. Instead of trying to change Dennis, she accepted his temperament and urged her husband to ease up on the boy.

PREDICTABILITY

We often confuse predictability with dependability. When we say someone is dependable, that means we know he will fulfill his obligations. But when we describe someone as predictable, we know what she will do when she's not under obligation.

I (Tim) live down the street from an older gentleman who is quite predictable; I can set my watch by the man's walks. His two-mile stroll happens at almost the same minute every afternoon. His wife, on the other hand, is unpredictable: one day she'll work in the garden, the next she'll ride her 1970s-style banana-seat bicycle, and the next day she'll sit quietly by the lake. This couple admits that their differences made things stressful early in their marriage, but over time they learned to accept each other's temperament.

PERSISTENCE

Contrary to the belief of go-getters, people who are more retiring are not deficient or doomed in life and work. Instead, they often find success in tasks that involve immediate goals and objectives, such as jobs where projects begin and are completed the same week or the same day. Administration, many sales jobs, some teaching positions, and plenty of other careers meet this criterion. Because of their people skills and ability to network, they can be very successful.

On the other hand, people who are extremely persistent are the driven types who transgress all barriers to succeed. They are diligent in the face of adversity and end up as CEOs, entrepreneurs, and partners in top law firms. They are strong-willed and often described as stubborn.

In order for both personalities to live in harmony, they need to accept each other as unique and not push one another to change. Persistent parents may be able to help their kids work toward a long-term goal and achieve great feats, but they will never mold them into being type-A personalities. Nonpersistent parents can use healthy techniques to help persistent kids to slow down over time, but their kids will always be driven.

MOOD

Mood is the foundation of a child's personality and can be observed even in newborns. Some babies are calm and joyful, and others are boisterous and adventurous. Some kids get easily rattled and upset, and others handle things with grace.

"Veronica, settle down," you might constantly tell your daughter. "Lower your voice; you're way too excited. You're at about a nine, and I need you at a five." But this exuberance may simply be Veronica's temperament, and by repeatedly critiquing her, you are communicating to your daughter that she is not acceptable.

Instead of trying to change her, foster an environment that helps her balance her moods by limiting her exposure to new adventures, trips to the toy store, and other adrenaline-inducing activities. As Veronica matures, she may mellow out. In the meantime, however, it's up to you to embrace her God-given energy while providing balance.

SENSORY THRESHOLD

Parents and children can have extremely different levels of

sensitivity when it comes to touch, smell, taste, hearing, and sight. Take the child who gets carsick and the parent who loves to drive! Or the kid who loves loud music and the parent who gets a migraine after five minutes of hearing loud bass. The parent who loves exotic foods and the child who can only stomach cheese pizza. Or the teen who wants to paint her room in magenta and silver and hang blinking Christmas lights in May and the mother who thinks beige is a bit daring. We could go on and on.

Not only do overcontrolling parents need to accept that their kids will have different opinions and emotions, but they also must realize their children have their own physical sensory threshold. Ethan may gag on hot sauce while the rest of his family puts jalapenos on everything, but that doesn't mean he's a wimp. Jessica may prefer to wave good-bye instead of giving you a hug at school, but that doesn't mean she loves you any less.

INTROVERSION VERSUS EXTROVERSION

Christina was sitting in the back booth of a local restaurant, celebrating her birthday with her family. Unlike a lot of teens, she was actually enjoying her time with her family. That is until her mom told the server that—"wink, wink"—it was Christina's birthday.

Minutes later, ten servers showed up at the table. One stood on top of a chair and bellowed, "We have a very special announcement to make tonight! It's Christina's seventeenth birthday! Let's everybody sing to her!"

As the servers sang their silly birthday song, banged pots

and pans, and motioned for everyone in the busy restaurant to join in, Christina sank further into the booth. The ordeal ruined the night for her—she felt exposed and taken advantage of. When they finally left the restaurant, Christina said tearfully, "That was totally embarrassing! I can't believe you did that to me, Mom."

Her mother's jaw dropped in surprise. "How could anyone not like that?" she asked. "And those guys were all so cute!"

As a quiet, somewhat timid teen, Christina simply couldn't take the attention her more outgoing family thrived on. She wanted to remain anonymous—especially on her birthday.

Like the rest of the traits we described, it's important to remain sensitive to where your kids fall on the spectrum, particularly if they differ from you. Take a moment to study the temperament chart to see where your child fits. Once you understand her temperament, you can begin to accept—rather than overcontrol—your child.

ROOM TO GROW

Christian child psychiatrist Grace Ketterman states, "Let me remind you: it is futile to try to change the inborn qualities of a child's temperament. The best you can do is to understand them, accept them, and gently help your child weave them into the unique, wonderful person she can become. Even the most difficult temperament reflects a valuable set of qualities."[4] Remember, God gave us the children He wanted us to have. He knew ahead of time what strengths and weaknesses, personality traits and habits, successes and challenges our kids would

TEMPERAMENT RATING SCALE[3]

Anxious	Laid back
Hurried	Slow paced
Irritable	Easy going
Quick tempered	Slow to anger
Jealous	Not envious
Overly sensitive	Tolerates teasing well
Embarrasses easily	Happy in the spotlight
Sulks often	Happy disposition
Dislikes challenges	Prefers challenges
Gives up easily	Perseveres
Serious	Funny
Inflexible	Adaptable
Dislikes change	Thrives on change
Breaks rules	Black and white
A loner	Social
Spiteful	Loving
Dislikes meeting new people	Enjoys meeting new people
Critical	Self-accepting
People pleaser	Independent thinker
Easily distracted	Concentrates well

possess. When we overcontrol, constantly criticizing or commanding our kids, we are stifling their God-given qualities.

God is the perfect parent. Just as He gives us, His children, the freedom to make mistakes, so must we also give our kids room to grow. We need to let our children express themselves, while still guiding them through the ups and downs of life-nurturing them for who they are, not who we want them to be.

part three

Connecting with Your Kids

LOVING YOUR CHILD
TOO MUCH

chapter ten

How Parents and Kids Connect

When Israel was a child, I loved him,
and out of Egypt I called my son . . . .

It was I who taught Ephraim to walk,
taking them by the arms . . . .

It was I who healed them. I led them with cords
of human kindness, with ties of love;

I lifted the yoke from their neck and bent
down to feed them.

Hosea 11:1–4

$\mathcal{G}$od created us to be in relationship with Him and others—with moms, dads, friends, acquaintances, distant cousins, aunts, uncles, siblings, business associates, and neighbors. Our closest relationships—what we call attachment relationships—have the most influence on who we are, what we do, and how we feel. We as parents are our kids' most important attachment figures. Usually moms are primary, with dads a close second. When our children trot off to school, their teachers become important attachment figures as well.

We can't understate the significance of attachment relationships. In fact, they are the reason we've written this book! When we give our kids unhealthy love—by overcontrolling, overprotecting, or overindulging—we are doing more than just damaging our own relationship with them. When we give our kids this toxic love, they don't receive the security and support that is needed to instill healthy attachment.

Intentionally or not, kids measure all their other relationships, both close and superficial, against the relationship they have with us, their attachment figures. If our relationship with them is generally healthy, they'll conclude that they are important and deserve love and protection. But if our relationship with them is characterized by toxic control, protection, or indulging, they may believe they are incapable of love or that others are out to quash their identity, manipulate them, or buy their love.

Kids carry these "relationship rules" with them through life as they venture into adolescence, dating, and marriage, deciding whether they'll be able to trust and receive love from their friends and family members, or whether those people will be emotionally distant, controlling, or rejecting. Parental relationships can also shape children's views of God. Is He a stern taskmaster who only cares about whether or not they obey Him? Or does He love and nurture them, making Himself available to them even in their darkest moments?

There are several important elements of healthy attachment. As you read, think about your relationship with your child. What things, either purposely or inadvertently, might you be teaching your child about relationships? Do you foster healthy attachment?

WHAT IS HEALTHY ATTACHMENT?

Where does your child turn when she's hurt? When the attachment is healthy, our kids usually turn to us. We are their secure bases—we enable them to live and thrive. When we are around, we give our children the confidence to explore their world and know that safety is close and available.

When this attachment is formed, beginning when children are about six months old, they begin to ask some critical questions. They wonder, *Is my mom nearby? Is she available to me? Will my dad be there for me? Can I get to him quickly if I need to?* When children reach four or five years old and are entering preschool or kindergarten, they no longer need to be physically close to us all the time—instead, they can conjure up a mental image of their mom or dad to calm them during times of stress. As long as they believe we'll be there if they really need us, most kids will face those first school experiences with relative calm. We may not be able to make their problems disappear, but even the promise of our presence and concern will help ease their pain.

When my (Gary) son, Jacob, was six, his baseball team practiced on a diamond that lay beside train tracks. Every few practices, the train roared past with a sudden explosion of thunderous sound. When the children heard the noise, then saw the train, they literally flew from the field like startled birds. Where did they run? To their parents, who ironically sat closer to the train itself!

God has programmed us to run to our attachment figures when we're upset. When our kids cry, scream, or run to us, they are signaling to us that something is wrong and they need our help. As children get older, they develop other ways of communicating. "Logan wouldn't play with me at recess," your eight-year-old son might tell you tearfully. "Anna's mad at me, and I don't know why," your teenage daughter might say. Other, less emotionally mature kids will act out their distress with misbehavior. They may seem to be distancing themselves with their acting out, but in reality they're desperately in need of our attention and support.

ATTACHMENT WOUNDS

Jim and Stella brought their seven-year-old son, Sammy, in for help with his temper tantrums. Sammy's fits had begun about seven or eight months ago. "Sammy has become increasingly difficult," explained Stella. "He argues about everything. He doesn't want to take a bath, go to bed, get dressed, or go to school.

"And if he doesn't get what he wants," she continued, "he falls on the floor, screams and flops around like a fish out of water. He's making us crazy. We don't know what to do!"

"Have you experienced any major life changes?" we asked. "Any stresses or crises?"

They had. Shortly before Sammy's problems began, his father, like many others in their town, had been laid off. Suddenly Stella had to work more hours, and Jim, who was at home looking for work, was depressed and angry. Before the layoff, Sammy had been his dad's "little buddy." They had done almost everything together. But since then, Jim, who was barely keeping his own head above water, had hardly talked to Sammy.

Predictably, Sammy started acting up—back-talking, pouting, and refusing to do what he was told. As Sammy's attitude became more and more rotten, his dad became increasingly frustrated. Soon Jim was either avoiding Sammy or yelling at him.

Finally after four months without a job, Jim had found one several hours away. Since a five-hour commute was impossible, he decided to stay near his job during the workweek and come home on the weekends. Instead of being happy to see his dad, though, Sammy avoided Jim when he arrived, refusing even to greet him when he came through the door.

"I can't stand to come home," admitted Jim. "I get this sick feeling in the pit of my stomach knowing that as soon as I walk through that door, Sammy's going to start up again. Lately, I've been trying to stay away from him. It seems like the more I'm around, the worse he behaves."

Sammy had suffered an attachment wound. His dad's abrupt unemployment had plunged the family into crisis, making his parents less emotionally available to him. He was scared and angry. And since he wasn't mature enough to voice these feelings, he was acting out by becoming defiant, throwing temper tantrums, and avoiding his father. His behavior was his way of saying, "Hey, what's going on? Don't you care about me anymore?"

When Jim left town during the week, the wound only deepened. Sammy believed that he had driven his dad away. His family's challenging financial situation meant nothing to him, and he had no idea that his behavior made his parents feel ineffective, helpless, and angry—normal behavior for a seven-year-old. All he really knew was that his difficult behavior got his parents' attention, and that negative attention was better than none at all.

Once we were able to identify the problem, Sammy's parents began to heal the attachment wound by changing how they dealt with their son. By making just a few crucial adjustments—which we'll explain later in the chapter—Jim and Stella were able to rebuild Sammy's confidence, and in a few months Sammy's symptoms had all but disappeared.

Sammy's story is far from unusual. Many, many children are suffering from what we call attachment wounds, or anything that seriously threatens the security of the attachment relationship. Attachment wounds can spring from obvious stress, such as intense marital conflict and divorce, or more subtle stress like family relocation, the birth of a sibling, or financial stress. Like Sammy, many of these kids feel abandoned in the wake of such stress. And it's no wonder: at no other time in history have more moms and dads worked outside the home, leaving their children with baby-sitters or home alone.

When parents are physically or emotionally absent,

children receive little of the normal stimulation, emotional soothing, or loving support parents provide. And if the parent is chronically absent, the child's ability to cope with problems, regulate their emotions, and develop a Christlike mind-set drops dramatically. Research by attachment expert John Bowlby shows that parental neglect deprives children of nurture and love and is, itself, a traumatic experience.[1]

Most of us at one time in our life remember getting briefly separated from our parents. Maybe we were in the grocery store or church, toddling ahead of our mom, when we looked back and saw that she was gone. We probably let out an ear-piercing scream and didn't stop howling until we were reunited with her. If even a momentary separation like that can cause distress, imagine what trauma kids experience when their parents are chronically absent, leaving their children in a constant state of neglect! As Sammy's story revealed, these kinds of attachment wounds are often the underlying reason children exhibit behavior problems.

Most parenting programs help parents become better disciplinarians. But for discipline to work effectively, we must have a strong relationship with our kids. When the security of our attachment relationship with our children is threatened, discipline seldom works. Instead of following their parents' rules, these children act out in fear and anger. "You better not leave me!" they say in effect, clinging to their parents. They need their parents back—available and accessible.[2]

Kids aren't the only ones affected. For instance, a husband tells his wife he'll be home from work at 6:00 p.m., but doesn't come through the door until 9:00 p.m. And since he doesn't call to let her know, she's wracked with anxiety and calls friends, family, and even the emergency room to see if he's there. Of course, once he comes home, her fear morphs into rage. Battling a mixture of anger and worry, she is suffering an attachment wound.

Being separated from our attachment figures causes a lot of anxiety. But when we lose important people in our life—if they die or become permanently unavailable—our anxiety can become unmanageable. We physically and emotionally shut down, losing motivation to do the things we used to enjoy. In adults, this hopelessness looks like classic depression, while children get grumpy and negative about everything, often becoming withdrawn and selfish.

This is normal behavior. After all, God created us to crave that closeness—with us and with Him. Fortunately, although things can happen to our attachment relationships on earth, the one we have with our heavenly Father will never change. We can take comfort in the Bible's reminder that "Jesus Christ is the same yesterday and today and forever" (Hebrews 13:8).

STRENGTHENING YOUR BOND IN TIMES OF STRESS

Families will experience stress. It's unavoidable! But it is possible to protect your children from attachment wounds, even when life seems to be spiraling out of control. If your family is experiencing job loss, a death in the family, divorce, illness, relocation, financial problems, or any other kind of stress, try following these suggestions:

KEEP THINGS STABLE AT HOME.

Do whatever you can to keep your home as a safe haven—a warm, familiar place with people and things around which make your kids comfortable. Serve meals at the usual times and in the usual ways, with the usual foods. Follow homework rituals, bath times, and bedtimes. And try to be home as much as possible, maintaining your usual roles, personality, and especially your sense of humor.

TELL YOUR KIDS WHAT'S GOING ON.

Many children get stressed because they are left in the dark. Their parents won't tell them what's going on, but they can see that things aren't quite right. They're on the outside playing detective.

Instead of protecting your kids, explain the circumstances in a way they can understand. First, give your child a summary of the situation, taking into account his maturity level. One mother explained, "Connor could see that something was wrong, and I didn't think it was right to hide it from him. So I sat him down next to me and told him I loved him, and that the reason things seemed strange is because Grandpa is very sick, and that he might die soon and leave us to go live in heaven with God."

Answer his questions honestly, and ask him if he has any other ones. Your child, needing to think through what you just told him, might say no but then return with more questions when he's ready. Connor's mother continued. "We both cried for a few minutes, and then I asked Connor if he had any questions. He asked, 'Does Grandpa have to die?' I told him that everyone dies someday, and I explained to him what that means. I also said we weren't sure exactly when Grandpa would die. Then I reminded him how much his grandpa loves him and how proud he is of him, and told Connor we would be leaving to see Grandpa that weekend."

Don't overwhelm the child with too much information too quickly. Kids can handle hard news, but they do it best in small doses. "Connor said he didn't have any more questions," his mom explained. "So I told him that whenever he did, he could come to me and I would answer them."

EMPHASIZE WHAT WILL NOT CHANGE.

Even when it seems like your whole world has turned upside down, the truth is that the majority of things have not changed. Point out to your child all the things that will stay the same. (This might comfort you too.) For instance, if you're moving to a new state, you can remind your daughter she will still have her own bedroom, the family will still be together, game night will still be every Sunday, and she'll still be able to do her favorite things like reading or taking dance lessons. There may even be some advantages, such as being closer to Grandma and Grandpa, having better weather, or having apple trees in the backyard.

REASSURE THEM THAT IT'S NOT THEIR FAULT.

When your family is experiencing a lot of stress, children take it all in. To complicate matters, kids think egocentrically like

Sammy did, meaning that they tend to think things happen *because* of them.

One beautiful spring evening, my wife, Lory, and I (Gary) were walking around the block with our two children, Jacob, seven, and Jordan, who was four. The sun was just starting to set, and the faded moon was hanging lazily in the sky. Jordan was fascinated by the moon, watching it out of the corner of her eye. If we turned left, she looked back at the moon, and if we turned right, she glared at it with squinted eyes. Finally, she whispered in a low, suspicious voice, almost as if she didn't want anyone else to hear her, "Dad . . . Dad! The moon's following us." Lory and I bit our lips and tried hard not to laugh as we explained to Jordan that it only looked like the moon was following us—it really wasn't. Jordan wasn't convinced. Somehow she thought that the moon would be interested in following us. Since it looked like it was, then it was.

Kids also use this kind of thinking when bad things occur, even when it seems ridiculous to adults. If dad drops a hammer on his toe and screams in pain, his children may believe they did something to cause him to be upset; and when parents fight or when their marriage tragically dissolves, children usually blame themselves. We can't count the number of children we've seen who blame themselves for their daddy leaving.

Therefore, reassure your children that the problems you're experiencing are not because of them. In fact, commend them for making the situation better. "Things are rough right now for the family," you might tell your son, "but I am so glad you're here, because your smile brings me sunshine every day."

SCHEDULE SPECIAL TIMES.

The key word here is *schedule*. During times of stress, it's easy to let fun activities take a backseat to more "important" and "necessary" tasks. But spending special time with your kids is more than just fun and games—it's extremely important. Schedule some fun activities together and take that time as seriously as you would any other important duty. You may find the time becomes a pretty important respite for you too. Even when special times need to be less frequent, scheduling gives kids specific events to look forward to. You might tell your kids, "We have to stay home tonight, but that's okay because we're going to the lake Saturday morning!"

BUILD SOME SPECIAL MOMENTS.

Many of us have a hard time giving anyone—including God, our spouses, and even ourselves—our undivided attention. So we often talk to parents about being "in the moment" with their kids. That is, giving your children your undivided, positive attention for a few minutes. During this time, try to listen to what your child is saying and make a concentrated effort to communicate to her. This tells her, "I really like you, and I'm interested in what you have to say."

These little bursts of connectedness may be brief, but they can be incredibly meaningful when done alongside a healthy, invested relationship. As one parent told us, "These special moments have become momentous occasions."

PROMOTING HEALTHY ATTACHMENT

If you tend to exhibit unhealthy love by overcontrolling, overindulging, or overprotecting, your attachment relationship with your child could be suffering. Overcontrolling parents tend to cause attachment wounds with their constant criticism and discipline. If their kids don't follow their instructions to the letter, these parents often withdraw out of frustration, further "punishing" their kids. Overindulgent parents who are chronically working or emotionally distant will shower their kids with gifts and toys to make up for their absence—just making their kids resentful and confused. And parents who overprotect inadvertently teach their children to trust no one, making it virtually impossible for their kids to form positive attachment relationships later in life.

Fortunately, although attachment styles are first formed in early childhood, it is never too late to strengthen your bond. It is possible to reshape your child's "rules" to promote healthy relationships.

chapter eleven

Building Closeness with Your Child

Home is for living and laughing. It should be a place we learn to play, to have fun, to relax. Make sure that the good ground of your home includes an abundance of laughter, parties, celebrations, presents, candles, Christmas trees, gifts, surprises, rocky road ice cream, jokes, backyard picnics, vacations, mountain hikes, bike rides, swimming, fishing, and games.

—Bill Carmichael, *Seven Habits of a Healthy Home*[1]

*F*ather thirst." That's what noted father expert, George Williams, calls the fruit of an absent dad. It's that emotionally unresolved and insatiable void that only a father can fill.[2]

We think that today kids suffer from "parent thirst." The true meaning of parent thirst hit home for me (Tim) when I was at one of my son's games. One of his teammates made a bad play and was embarrassed in front of his buddies. Upset, the boy ran toward the stands to look for his mom's support. Instead of finding her watching with everyone else, he finally discovered her off to the side of the bleachers on her cell phone. The poor kid was inconsolable. He looked down the sideline toward his mother and screamed, "GET OFF THE PHONE! GET OFF THE PHONE! GET OFF THE PHONE!" As the young boy yelled, his coaches ran over to try to calm him down.

"What would she do if she was off the phone?" one of them asked.

"She'd talk to *me!*" he cried.

When your children know you're not "all there," they believe it's because you don't care about them. And when they see you in the stands on your cell phone, PDA, or just looking at the clouds planning your next big deal, they tell themselves, *I'm just not that important to you. And since you're my parent, I must not be that important to anyone.*

In all our years of teaching, counseling, ministering, and now parenting, we cannot say enough about the significance and power of parenting. God has clearly designed the family as an incubator for shaping our kids' hearts and minds about life and love. As each child grows in the protective environment of the home, this attachment provides him with a sense of security and trust, key ingredients for healthy relationships.

But in most homes across America, kids are being parented largely by television and video games, taking in about nine hours a day of media. Sadly, we may have become the first generation of parents to be widely unavailable to our children. Most parents agree that there just isn't enough time in the day to meet all of life's demands. And the inevitable losers of this life in the fast lane are our kids.

Even if parents are physically present, they are often emotionally and socially absent from their kids.[3] For example, in his book *The Father Factor and the Two-Parent Advantage,* Henry Biller found that fewer than 25 percent of young boys and girls experience at least an hour per day in one-on-one contact with their fathers. Overall, it's more like thirty minutes per day,[4] and as time goes on, one-on-one contact with moms is growing equally sparse.

Bill Hybels, pastor of Willow Creek Community Church, says, "Hurried men skim life, skim wife, and skim kids."[5] And hurried parents pass these traits on to their children. According to a recent study, children who are not nurtured properly by their parents often lack the skills to parent their own kids in turn.[6]

One teenager we met with described himself as having "in-between parents." He explained that his parents were hard-working, well-intentioned people who try and squeeze good parenting in between all the other necessary things they need to do. But most kids aren't quite as perceptive as this teen. They don't understand that their parents are neglecting them because they're busy trying to give their kids a good life. They simply feel neglected and rejected.

It wasn't always this way. In the past, child-rearing was acknowledged as an important part of life. "Family comes first" was a common mantra that fathers and mothers would recite to escape overtime at work or other burdening demands on their time. Families may not have had plasma televisions—or even televisions at all—and they may have lived in smaller homes, but children more often had the presence of two stable parents when they arrived home from school or shortly thereafter.

In the past, raising children was considered an important, honorable task, one worth the sacrifices involved. But somewhere, somehow all this changed. Not too long ago, Ann Landers asked her readers if they would choose again to be parents. Shockingly, 70 percent of the fifty thousand people who replied said that they would not have children if they were given the opportunity to live their life over! To the majority, raising children is no longer a privilege and a gift from God to be cherished. For many, it is at best status quo.

The Old Testament directs parents, "Love the LORD your God with all your heart and with all your soul and with all your strength. These commandments that I give you today are to be upon your hearts. Impress them on your children. Talk about them when you sit at home and when you walk along the road, when you lie down and when you get up" (Deuteronomy 6:5–7). The bottom line is that parents are to nurture and guide their children, despite the sacrifices of time, money, luxury, or independence.

While we believe that most parents deeply love their children and want the best for them, often their message of love is simply not getting through. Kids spell love T-I-M-E. Our children yearn for our responses, our presence, our ability to set limits, and the assurance that we can be trusted and will be there for them.

Perhaps it is unfortunate that parents cannot simply "buzz in" and build a meaningful relationship in the minutes between job number 1 and job number 2. If that were the case, we would have much less to write! We can't just overindulge them to ease our guilt, throwing toys and gifts at them in hopes that they know we love them. And contrary to popular belief, it's not just about quality time—it's about quantity of time. It's about praying with them before bedtime, getting drinks of water in the middle of the night, and listening to our kids' dreams the next morning. It's about the moments that show up unexpectedly, only after hours and hours of just being together.

EMOTIONAL BANK ACCOUNTS

All close relationships have an emotional bank account. The emotional quality of this account comes from the relationship we have with that person. We need to know that our attachment figures are there for us—no matter what—and that if we need them in times of trouble, they will be available and willing to help us. In our relationships, we make deposits into our emotional accounts when we do things that communicate love, concern, warmth, and interest.

Spending time together is the best kind of deposit you can make. Throwing the baseball with your son, playing dolls with your daughter, or going for a walk are examples of bonding with your child. While these may seem like small deposits, they are not! They say to your child, "I care about you, and I'm here for you if you need me."

We make withdrawals on the account whenever there is conflict or stress in the relationship. For example, when we disagree with our spouse about parenting issues or money, or when we correct our child's language, set firm limits for bedtime or television time, or take away a privilege because of backtalk. Similarly, we also make withdrawals on the account when we give our kids unhealthy love through overprotecting, overindulging, or overcontrolling.

The goal is to keep the account balance positive and to never overdraw it by making too many withdrawals and too few deposits. When the account gets overdrawn, stress in the relationship increases. Negative feelings grow stronger, and we begin questioning each other's motives. For instance, a child whose relationship with his mom is strained might say, "Mom, you're just making rules to ruin my life!" As trust erodes, the relationship becomes increasingly troubled. Neither party budges, leaving the relationship deadlocked in conflict. Eventually, if the bank account stays negative long enough, relational bankruptcy will occur. When this happens, the mother may feel angry and resentful toward her child, worn out by the constant battles and negativity. "My son's just being a brat!" she might say, tempted to emotionally and physically withdraw from him.

But children misinterpret their parents' anger, resentment, and emotional withdrawal as abandonment. They often struggle with feeling they can't do anything right, telling themselves, *No matter what I do, Mom and Dad are always mad at me.* They fail to see the connection between their misbehavior and their parents' anger and frustration. They believe their mom and dad are angry with them as people. *Something is wrong with me*, they think, and they begin to question their attachment relationship. *I can't count on my parents; they don't care about me.*

Parents need to know their children can think like this, even though it's usually not true. Understandably, parents get upset when they discover their children feel this way. "She must know that's not true!" they say. "We love Rachel; she can come to us at any time." While that may be true, it's important to remember that our children tune into our emotions and behaviors more than to our actual words.

Susan, a twenty-eight-year-old mother of three, looked defeated and exhausted the first time she stepped into our office with her eight-year-old son, Dillon, in tow. As she recounted her problems with Dillon, her tone grew increasingly negative.

"He's never happy unless he's making somebody else miserable," she complained. "He picks on his younger sister until she blows up at him. When I tell him to leave her alone, he goes off like dynamite. He stomps his feet and screams at me. And discipline does nothing. I yell, I scream, I take things away, I ground him, I spank him . . . absolutely nothing works. He just gets even more determined to defy me. And Dillon is just as bad, maybe even worse with his dad."

We listened closely to Susan's story and then asked, "Susan, are there times when Dillon isn't acting up or when you actually enjoy being with him?"

"Not really," she said, frowning. "The only time he behaves is when he's trying to get something. Then he can be sugary sweet. But I don't give in to that. I know what he's up to."

"What do you do when he gets sweet like that?" we asked.

"I either ignore him or I call his bluff. 'Dillon,' I tell him, 'if you're being nice just because you're trying to get something, you might as well give it up, because you're not getting it!'"

"What does Dillon do when you call his bluff?"

Susan's face hardened. "He turns back into the real Dillon—smarting off and getting into trouble." She took a deep breath and let it out slowly. "Nothing works with him. I really don't know what to try next."

Like many parents, Susan had reached relational bankruptcy with Dillon. She felt helpless and angry. And the more unimpressed Dillon appeared by his mother's anger, the more frustrated Susan became.

The biggest problem, however, was Susan's negative perception of her son. As she described Dillon's behavior, she used words like "always," "never," and "constantly"—a sure sign the relationship was in trouble. Her negative thinking also caused her to selectively ignore Dillon's good behavior. The only time Dillon behaved, according to Susan, was when he wanted something. This, of course, only made Susan resent Dillon more—which in turn only strengthened Dillon's conviction that nothing he did could please his mom.

Susan had tried several discipline strategies, all to no avail. High-powered tactics like spankings, time-outs, and removing privileges only caused Dillon's behavior to worsen. He didn't care if he crashed and burned. He only wanted to get back at his mother!

Fortunately, there are ways to mend even the most broken relationships. As we talked with Susan and Dillon, we guided them through several key steps that would help restore the balance.

KEEP IT POSITIVE

To keep the balance in your account positive, it's crucial you find ways to keep making deposits—especially when your kids are misbehaving or you're dealing with a difficult child. As these positive experiences add up, you'll find that your children are more motivated to please you and that your discipline techniques work more effectively.

Begin by setting aside approximately twenty minutes to play with your child. This should be a one-on-one interaction that excludes friends, siblings, or other family members. Your children will appreciate even this small gesture of "special time." Many parents live such time-starved lives they hardly sit down to dinner, let alone take the time to play.

For banking time to be effective, it must be consistent. We suggest a minimum of three to four sessions per week. Children—even those who seem to love chaos—seek predictability in their relationships. When you're consistent with this time, your kids will begin to look forward to the event—an important step in the relationship-rebuilding phase. For children under nine, it's best to schedule that time every day. With older children, we recommend that you simply join them in play.

Make sure your sessions are not contingent on your child's behavior. Let your child know that he cannot earn special time, and he cannot lose it either. Don't worry—doing this will not reward defiant behavior since the sessions are planned in advance. Placing contingencies on this time with your child can actually damage the relationship and increase the chance that he will act out.

Before your first playtime, sit down with her and explain that you want to begin setting aside a few minutes several times a week for just the two of you. Then brainstorm some activities you can do together. Encourage her to pick activities that she likes—ones that can last about twenty to thirty minutes and don't include television. Video games can be appropriate, even if you're simply watching and cheering her on. And if she wants to play a two-person video game, hop in and join her.

During the banking time session, don't ask intrusive questions and don't give commands. This may be difficult to do if you struggle with overcontrol, but intrusive questions and commands will only interfere with play, increasing the odds that she will become defiant. Don't use the time for moral instruction either. There are plenty of other times you can teach and instruct your child. If your child does misbehave, try to ignore the behavior and avoid eye contact, or, if necessary, end the banking session. Above all, relax and enjoy yourself! Remember, the goal is to connect with your child. Follow her lead. This is a powerful way of communicating to her that she is loved.

You can also try observing your child's play and describing what you see—much like a sportscaster providing commentary or a reporter telling a story: "Ryan pushes the car across the floor, and it crashes into a pile of wadded-up paper balls." "Wow! Adriana just threw the tennis ball for her dog, Tucker, and it bounced all the way across the lawn!" Young kids love this. When adults get involved in their playtime, they feel important and liked.

Look for something special and unique about your child, and point those qualities out. But when you do, be very specific about what it is that you like. For example, you might say, "I like the way you straightened up your dollhouse, Maggie." You could also notice her good behavior and tell her, "Thank you for sharing your dolls with me!" Avoid making general statements like, "You're such a good girl." When kids don't know *why* they're "good," they can get confused and anxious.

Keep a log of your banking time sessions, recording when you did it, what you did, for how long, and what positive thing you learned about your child. This log does a couple of important things. First, it keeps you accountable. Oftentimes parents will try to convince themselves that they did special time when in fact they only thought about doing it. Second, the log helps you stay positive. Discovering new and pleasant things about your child will go a long way toward improving your feelings about him. There is usually a direct correlation between how many positive things parents discover about their child and the overall improvement in his behavior.

At the end of each week, review these logs prayerfully. If you're having difficulty finding the time for these sessions, ask God to help you reevaluate your priorities and make some tough decisions about how you're spending your time. If you need some assistance with time management, consult a friend, counselor, or pastor.

Also, if you can't find anything positive about your kids, ask the Lord to help you see things differently. The Bible says, "Whatever is true, whatever is noble, whatever is right, whatever is pure, whatever is lovely, whatever is admirable—if anything is excellent or praiseworthy—think about such things" (Philippians 4:8). Be open with Him about your struggle—God can help you see the good in even the most challenging people.

For parents with a history or tendency to overprotect, overcontrol, or overindulge, banking time is vital because it reverses the stresses on the relationship. In time, these banking sessions will enable you to have a healthy relationship from which you can discipline more effectively as you set firm, clear limits and commands and use logical, natural consequences. These sessions will also enable you to model and teach morals and values to your kids. Through these special times, you'll be able to harness the most powerful resource you have for teaching your kids to live, love, and grow in the Lord—your relationship.

chapter twelve

Emotion Coaching

Family life is our first school for emotional learning.

—Daniel Goleman, *Emotional Intelligence*[1]

*E*motional intelligence sounds like "jumbo shrimp"—an oxymoron, doesn't it? It's not. Emotional intelligence is the ability to understand and regulate our emotions. To know when we're feeling angry, for instance, and then to express that anger appropriately. Or to realize when we're jealous, and to know how to handle our envy. Emotional intelligence also helps us understand other people's feelings and respond to them sensitively and respectfully. It helps us know when someone else is upset with us and to acknowledge that person's feelings and deal with their emotions in a healthy way.

Many of the parents who come to our offices tell us their kids are out of control—emotionally volatile and rebellious, constantly acting out. These parents ask, "Why? What makes my child so much harder to handle than other kids his age?"

Children with behavior problems are not necessarily "bad kids." And, parents of children with behavior problems are not necessarily "bad parents." In our experience, they're often suffering from an inability to regulate their emotions.

As family-focused counselors, we've found that we often help parents most by teaching them how to build emotional intelligence in their children. Observations of early parent-child interactions and infant sleep patterns reveal that some children seem to have the ability to control their emotions from birth, while other kids need coaching to improve their emotional intelligence.

What Is Emotion Coaching?

"Keep those arms going in the same direction you're running. If you move them across the front of your body, it'll slow you down. Concentrate on your arms for the next few miles, and after that it'll be natural. You'll see." This coach is doing his job, helping his athlete learn how to run faster.

Emotion coaching essentially does the same thing: teaching children how to deal with anger, disappointment, fear, excitement, and the other emotions we all experience in life. As we've seen, parents who overcontrol, overprotect, or overindulge often inadvertently try to eliminate these unhealthy symptoms. Instead of teaching their kids to work through those feelings, they want to suppress them. Left unregulated, however, these emotions can produce unhealthy symptoms of behavior. For instance, anger can produce defiance; and sorrow or anxiety can produce depression, withdrawal, and dependence.

Kids who receive emotion coaching from their parents experience fewer negative feelings. They're more resilient. They may get angry, sad, irritated, and disappointed, but they can control those emotions and behave appropriately. This type of coaching also helps kids deal with issues such as divorce, moving, changing schools, sickness, and loss. According to relationship expert John Gottman:

> When the Emotion-Coaching parents in our studies experienced marital conflict, or were separated or divorced, something different happened. . . . Emotion-Coaching seemed to shield them [their kids] from the deleterious effects suffered by so many who have this experience. Previously proven effects of divorce and marital conflict, such as academic failure, aggression, and problems with peers, did not show up in the Emotion-Coached kids; all of which suggests that Emotion-Coaching offers children the first proven buffer against the emotional trauma of divorce.[2]

And there are other benefits:

CHILDREN WITH PARENTS WHO
USE EMOTIONAL COACHING[3]

Have superior physical and emotional health
Score better academically
Get along better with others
Have fewer behavior problems

Are less prone to violence
Are able to tolerate negative feelings
Focus on the positive
Are better prepared for spiritual growth

TEACHING EMOTIONAL AWARENESS

Eleven-year-old Jaime came home from soccer practice in tears. Her mother looked up from her cookbooks and frowned. "What is it?"

"Em . . . Emma said she h . . . hates me," Jaime told her mom, sobbing. "She isn't my best friend anymore."

"Oh, don't worry about it," her mom said, continuing to prepare dinner. "That's just kid stuff."

Jaime slumped into the kitchen chair and buried her face in her hands. Her dad, who was chopping onions, stopped, walked over to Jaime, and stroked her hair. "Honey," he said, "that must hurt very much. I'm so sorry that happened to you."

As Jaime's dad illustrated, emotion coaching is more than just getting your child to name her feelings—it's also about relating to her. If Jamie had walked in angry, slamming the door and mumbling under her breath, her dad could have taken the same approach. When a child is visibly agitated, simply stopping and asking why she's upset can create an opportunity to connect with her. The goal is to listen, not provide solutions or keep her from feeling pain.

Stop what you're doing and pay attention to your child's behavior. Ask questions. Listen. Give your child a hug. Once she feels understood, she'll naturally begin the problem-solving process. You might ask, "How are you going to handle this?" Be sure not to take over the process, though. Offer support, but give advice cautiously. You might also share similar experiences you had as a kid and describe ways you dealt with them, both good and bad. And remember that your child's feelings are just as powerful and important as yours.

Of course, none of this will work if you don't take responsibility for your own feelings and behaviors. Emotion coaching is no different from the rest of parenting: your kids will learn much more from your actions than your words. The famous psychologist Lev Vygotsky called this "scaffolding" and used the illustration of kids building around their parents' foundation and strength.[4] When parents are healthy themselves, their kids will learn to calm themselves and problem-solve—maturing and stretching all the while.

This is why if you struggle with loving your child too much by overprotecting, overcontrolling, or overindulging, it's absolutely imperative that you focus on changing that behavior in addition to trying the techniques we've discussed. All the emotion coaching, banking time, and good discipline strategies in the world will not help your relationship with your kids unless you are modeling and building a foundation of healthy love.

Start by taking responsibility for your own actions and emotions and stop playing the blame game.[5] If you want to teach your kids how to regulate their feelings, you can't blame your spouse or your children for the way you feel or for how you react. You can't tell them, "You made me lose my temper!" or "You're working on my last nerve!"

You must also treat your kids with respect. Simply punishing them or treating them with disrespect—fighting fire with fire[6]—won't work. If Brian yells, it won't help the situation to yell louder. He may listen temporarily, but screaming or blaming or becoming vindictive is no way to build a relationship or to teach him a Christlike mind-set. Kids may have trouble regulating their emotions, but we as adults need to keep it together. We need to learn to keep our cool and continually act in a calm, loving manner, even while our children argue, fight, and disobey.

We've listed some other basic tips to help you get started:

EMOTION COACHING TIPS

Get to know yourself. The better you understand your own emotions, the better you'll understand your child's.
Try to see the world through her eyes.
Display the emotions you want your child to exhibit; treat him with the kindness you want him to show others.
Share your emotions and experiences with him.
Help her identify complex feelings. Does she feel indignant? Grieved? Arrogant? Vindictive? Vulnerable? Violated?
Help him discover where his feelings come from.
Validate your child's feelings. Acknowledge and explore them with patience and understanding.

Pay attention to his emotions throughout the day and note when he's upset or angry. Work on these situations with him.
Encourage her to talk about her emotions. Let her know that you're paying attention and taking her seriously.
Always empathize before giving advice.
Instead of telling your child what he ought to feel, help him identify what he's feeling.

TEACHING A CHRISTLIKE MIND-SET

Emotion coaching helps us do more than just keep a handle on our feelings. It also allows us to develop our spiritual side. It is only when we are calm and rational with our feelings that we can foster a Christlike mind-set. The apostle Paul wrote, "Do nothing out of selfish ambition or vain conceit, but in humility consider others better than yourselves" (Philippians 2:3). If our anger is out of control, or we're vengeful, we certainly can't put Paul's instructions into practice.

Developing this kind of humility isn't just a matter of willpower. It takes enormous empathy and insight, and the ability to endure pain. But by emotionally coaching our children, we can help them develop a Christlike mind-set. Take a few minutes to study the checklist to see how your child's doing.

Of course, developing a Christlike attitude requires us to turn from our sin. And resisting sin is actually linked to controlling our emotions! The Bible states, "The acts of the sinful nature are obvious: sexual immorality, impurity and debauchery;

DOES YOUR CHILD HAVE A CHRISTLIKE MIND-SET?

MY CHILD	ALWAYS	SOMETIMES	NEVER
Takes into consideration the concerns and feelings of others (Matthew 7:12)			
Shows compassion (Mark 1:41)			
Can delay gratification (Matthew 4:1–4)			
Can problem-solve (Matthew 22:15–22)			
Will negotiate with others (John 8:7)			
Is flexible (John 2:1–8)			
Can control strong emotions (Mark 14:35–36)			
Is slow to anger (Matthew 26:40–45)			
Is able to experience joy in the moment (John 21:12–13)			
Is able to tolerate discomfort (Matthew 27:32–44)			
Is growing spiritually (John 20:21–22)			

idolatry and witchcraft; hatred, discord, jealousy, fits of rage, selfish ambition, dissensions, factions and envy; drunkenness, orgies, and the like. I warn you, as I did before, that those who live like this will not inherit the kingdom of God. But the fruit of the spirit is love, joy, peace, patience, kindness, goodness, faithfulness, gentleness and self-control. Against such things there is no law" (Galatians 5:19–23).

A good portion of the sin we commit comes from the choices we make as we attempt to soothe our discomfort. For example, people who use illegal drugs are trying to ease their emotional pain. People who are sexually impure are often trying to fulfill unmet emotional needs. If we hope to minimize our sin, we must see God as our ultimate source of emotional comfort instead of booze, drugs, sex, food, or any other substitute.

We will all experience pain—we can't overprotect our kids from every instance of suffering. But when we do, our faith in God and the promise of heaven can help make our suffering bearable. The Bible says, "We know that the whole creation has been groaning as in the pains of childbirth right up to the present time. Not only so, but we ourselves, who have the firstfruits of the Spirit, groan inwardly as we wait eagerly for our adoption as sons, the redemption of our bodies" (Romans 8:22–23).

Our suffering will come to an end one day, and what a day it will be to see Christ ascending on the wings of glory! When we understand that our suffering is for a purpose and is temporary, we can endure it. By emotionally coaching our kids, we can help them learn to cope with and tolerate negative feelings, teaching them how God uses our pain to help us grow and mature.

chapter thirteen

Effective Discipline for Any Child

Those whom I love I rebuke and discipline.

Revelation 3:19

As family counselors, we see it all: the sarcastic and rude child. The girl who continually cuts class. The boy who hits the other kids in day care. The high school senior who stays out until midnight each night, smoking and drinking with his friends. The teen who backtalks and curses at his parents. When parents bring their kids in to our offices, it's often because they're facing major problems such as these. Sometimes they've been disciplining their kids for years, following good advice, and nothing seems to be working. Often they're frustrated and at their wits' end. And usually, they believe they are bad parents. After all, good kids always come from good parents, and defiant kids come from bad parents—right?

But this notion is one of parenting's longest-running and most destructive beliefs. Sometimes parents who are struggling with out-of-control kids are actually doing a lot of things right! In fact, parents of well-behaved kids might actually be locked into patterns of overcontrolling, overindulging, or overprotecting.

"How could that be?" you might ask. The answer is often temperament.

Temperament is a character trait that affects the most basic aspects of who we are, what we do, and how we do things. It defines our activity level, adaptability, attention span, mood, eating habits, sleep cycles, and the ability to regulate our emotions. Every child is born with a unique, God-given temperament—one that we must understand and accept before we can begin to discipline him.

Even in infancy, most children can be classified into one of four general temperament categories:

EASY KIDS

Easy kids seem to be able to control their emotions almost from birth. Most of the time they are even-tempered, relaxed, and positive. They adapt to feeding and sleeping schedules with grace, and are flexible when they miss a nap or a snack. They have good attention spans and are a pleasure to be around. They are the babies that everyone wants to hold and play with.

As older kids, these children have less trouble getting out of bed for school, following instructions and getting along with others in class, and calming down or focusing enough after school to do their homework. To use a baseball analogy, these kids are like pitchers who lob baseballs. With easy kids, parents can look like superstars, occasionally swinging hard and straight at the ball to hit it right out of the park.

DIFFICULT KIDS

Unlike easy kids, children with difficult temperaments are much more experienced "pitchers." They will throw fastballs, curveballs, and knuckleballs, and the same parents who look like superstars with easy kids may look like rookies when they're up against a challenging child.

These children are fussy, grumpy, and generally negative. With these kids, there's no such thing as a predictable schedule, because they have trouble adapting to eating and sleeping patterns. They may be easily distracted, and their level of activity is often inappropriate for the situation, making them a menace of teachers and a common fixture in the principal's office. For instance, they may be hyper in the morning, withdrawn during the day, and keyed up again at bedtime. This behavior is often misunderstood as "delinquency" and "spoiledness." These kids may simply be strong-willed or temperamental, or they may have diagnosable behavioral problems such as ADHD or ODD (Oppositional Defiance Disorder).

SLOW-TO-WARM-UP KIDS

These kids don't adjust well to people and new environments. Like difficult kids, they can be negative, especially during times of change. But when kids who are slow to warm up get comfortable with their environment, schedule, and the general goings-on, they resemble easy kids. The key in working with these kids is consistency. Wise parents will observe consistent sleep and eating schedules so as not to jostle them, and control the number of strangers and unfamiliar situations they are exposed to at any given time.

For instance, Terri's five-year-old son, Matthew, has a slow-to-warm-up temperament, while Terri does not. Every morning Terri leaps from bed and scrambles downstairs in an upbeat mood. It's not unusual to hear her humming as she heads for her coffeemaker. Matthew, on the other hand, needs several reminders and a lot of encouragement to get him up. He doesn't talk much—in fact, he seems to wake up with a permanent scowl—until he's had a chance to shovel down a bowl of cereal and stare at the games on the back of the box. Terri longs to chat with her son because morning is her favorite time of the day, but she knows she won't get any response from Matthew until he's good and ready. So she tries to keep her questions to a minimum, follows the same routine each morning, and turns down the volume on the TV in order to avoid upsetting her more sensitive child.

MIXED-TEMPERAMENT KIDS

This fourth category is not an exclusive "type" but instead a reminder that not all kids fit neatly into one category. Many are a unique combination of all three. Similar to slow-to-warm-up kids, mixed-temperament kids often change depending on their environment. For instance, your child might be a joy unless she is tired, sick, or stressed. When things don't go quite her way, she may quickly spiral into one difficult and moody kid!

ONE SIZE DOES NOT FIT ALL

Since not all kids are the same, parents must be willing to adapt their parenting style—and methods of discipline—to fit their child's personality and God-given traits. Good parents don't believe the myth that "all kids need the same kind of parenting." We cannot stress enough how critical this point is.

What's interesting about this myth is that sometimes mental-health professionals are the people who perpetuate it the most. I (Gary) have come across Christian professionals who preach about "God's way" for raising kids—providing a parenting recipe that is said to work for every child—and I've also met secular therapists with similar behavioral-style approaches to raising "perfect" kids. This type of philosophy is appealing to a lot of parents, because it promises easy methods and quick fixes. And many of these approaches can be very effective, although they usually only work on kids with easy temperaments.

The truth is that each of our kids is a complex creation, and often our parenting strategies have to be just as nuanced in order to work. We must become students of our kids and committed prayer warriors, adjusting our approach as needed.

Some parents get a little defensive when we suggest that they adjust their style and seek the cooperation of their kids.

But this is a biblical principle. Scripture teaches, "Train up a child in the way he should go, and when he is old he will not turn from it" (Proverbs 22:6). The Amplified Bible translates the phrase "in the way he should go" as "keeping with his individual gift or bent." Other translations interpret the phrase to be "*according to the ways of the Lord.*" We like both interpretations, because we've learned that no two children are the same, and no one method of discipline and correction will work for everyone. What should stay consistent, however, is the love and respect we communicate to each of the kids God entrusts to our care.

One mother I (Gary) know from church and deeply admire told me, "Dr. Sibcy, I've raised five children, and they are so different. I can't parent one like I parent the other. It's as if with every one of my kids I had to learn to become a parent all over again!"

In the following pages, we've outlined several discipline techniques, including "attention" and "ignoring," and the basic forms of correction. As you read, keep your child's temperament in mind. You, the parent, will know best what techniques will be most successful with your child. It is only when you understand and affirm your child's God-given temperament that your discipline will be effective.

THE POWER OF POSITIVE ATTENTION

A raise. A trophy. An award for a job well done. A simple "thank you." A spoken "I love you." A high five or a smile. These all speak to our need for approval and acknowledgement.

When we counsel parents, we often ask them why they think their children misbehave. "Because they want attention," most of them say, scowling or sighing. The implication is that their kids' desire for attention is immature or unhealthy. But we believe God created us to want attention, to be needed. Our brain seems wired for it!

The Bible is full of people who sought after God, wanting His attention and approval. Throughout his writings, King David basked in God's love, pleaded for His mercy, and begged for His forgiveness. And he didn't give up. He asked God to hear him dozens and dozens of times! "Listen to my prayer, O God," begged David, "do not ignore my plea; hear me and answer me" (Psalm 55:1–2). His psalms are filled with songs, praises, prayers, and meditations, all seeking God's help, attention, mercy, and love.

We are no different from King David. We all need and want the attention of our heavenly Father. We all want to hear God say to us someday, "Well done, good and faithful servant!" And amazingly, the God of the universe wants to hear from us! Scripture makes it clear that God actually wants us—His children—to seek Him out and to crave His attention. So why should it be any different for earthly parents and children?

When it comes to molding behavior, positive attention can be just as powerful as the most effective forms of discipline. To drive home our point, we recently asked Sally, the mother of a defiant six-year-old, about her experiences with bosses. Not surprisingly, Sally described one of her "bad" bosses as critical, overcontrolling, and demeaning.

"If I made a mistake," she explained, "Bob jumped all over

me. He made such a big deal about it, and he would put me down in front of everyone. In staff meetings, he spent most of his time on what we were doing wrong, and he did it almost mockingly. That really hurt."

"Why do you think it made you feel so badly?" we asked.

"Well, he was right. We made mistakes. But he never paid attention to what we did right. It seemed like he just waited for us to mess up so he could pounce. When we did well, which was most of the time, he just ignored us.

"I guess he believed that if he pointed out our mistakes, he would help us make fewer of them," she continued thoughtfully. "But it only made us angry. Some people got so angry they resigned. Others just stopped trying."

After a few minutes of continued chatting, we moved on. "How about 'good' bosses, Sally?"

"Well, the one I have now is pretty good," she said.

"What makes her such a good boss?"

"She's very clear about what she wants. That makes it easier, because you know where the line is."

"What happens if you cross the line?"

"She will definitely let you know," Sally continued. "She's very direct and firm when it comes to things like being on time, meeting deadlines, and acting professionally."

We ventured, "It sounds like she's pretty tough."

"She is, but she's good at recognizing our strengths. If we make mistakes, she lets us know and then quickly starts encouraging us again."

"Does she acknowledge your work?"

"Definitely," Sally said. "Just the other day I turned in a report. I worked hard on it, staying up most of the night. Later that day she came to my office and complimented me, saying, 'Sally, this is really good stuff. It looks like you put a lot of effort into this. Thanks.' There were some minor errors in it, but she didn't let that stop her from giving me some good, positive feedback."

"Does her style of supervision affect your work performance?" we asked.

"It feels good to have someone acknowledge your hard work. When someone is interested in you as a person and genuinely seems to care about your successes—it really makes a difference. You don't miss as much work, you show up on time, and you're more productive. You want to work hard for her."

As Sally's experience indicated, positive attention can powerfully and effectively mold behavior. Just as her good boss did, you, too, can use attention to help your child learn better ways to behave. There are two kinds of behavior: *Okay behavior* consists of things you want to see more of, like good manners, self-control, or using an "inside voice" when appropriate. Meanwhile, *not okay behavior* includes things you'd like your child to stop, like whining, interrupting, pouting, and minor forms of misbehavior. (This doesn't include dangerous behavior such as destroying property, hurting others, and stealing.)

To modify your child's behavior, we recommend using two kinds of responses: *attention* and *ignoring*. The goal is to give positive attention to her okay behavior and to ignore her not-okay behavior. When you attend to and praise your child, you'll see more of her okay behavior. This is no big surprise to most parents. But if you ignore your child's okay behavior, you'll actually see less of it.

This is a vital point. Many parents of defiant kids believe it is better to let sleeping dogs lie. They worry that if they pay attention to their child's good behavior it will stir up trouble. As one parent said, "If I catch William playing quietly in his room and I say anything to him, he immediately starts whining and demanding that I do stuff for him, which brings on a battle. So I just let him be. I don't want to spoil a few precious moments of silence."

William's mom makes an important point. In the short run, paying attention to okay behavior may actually prompt him to start misbehaving. Why? Because he's learned that acting up is the best way of holding her attention, even though it's negative. In the long run, however, attending to good conduct will motivate him to continue his good behavior.

When you only handle your child's not-okay behavior by correcting, criticizing, and complaining about it, you'll see more of it. Many parents believe that by doing this, they are disciplining or punishing their child and minimizing bad behavior. Unfortunately, it works just the opposite. Think back to Sally's "bad boss." The more he criticized his employees, the more poorly they worked. He couldn't see how he was reinforcing negative work performance.

On the other hand, when you ignore not-okay behavior, you'll see less of it. Of course, sometimes your kid's behavior will get worse before it gets better, especially if you first yelled or complained and then tried to ignore it. For instance, if your daughter constantly tugs at your arm when she wants to leave church and you used to yell at her for it, ignoring will initially make her try even harder for your attention. But eventually, ignoring will work. Like many things in life and parenting, it just takes patience and persistence.

ATTENDING AND PRAISING OKAY BEHAVIOR	CORRECTING AND CRITICIZING NOT-OKAY BEHAVIOR
Results in more okay behavior	Results in more not okay behavior
IGNORING OKAY BEHAVIOR	IGNORING NOT-OKAY BEHAVIOR
Results in less okay behavior	Results in less not-okay behavior[1]

ATTENDING AND PRAISING

Giving your child positive attention for okay behavior can have a powerful effect. In fact, sometimes it can turn around the entire relationship! The first method we teach is *attending*. If you've been doing banking time sessions with your child, you've already been using this skill. You use "attends" when you describe what your child is doing in a play-by-play fashion: "You're stacking all the blocks . . . You're pushing the big red truck across the floor. It crashes into the pile of blocks!"

Children, especially between ages three and eight, love this kind of attention. The key is to only describe compliant behavior. So if your child is crashing the truck into the pile of blocks, and this is pretend play, then you should attend to it. Pretend play is good, even if it includes minor violence, because kids need to learn how to use play—instead of their fists or other aggressiveness—to express their anger or frustration. If your child is just being a little destructive, though, ignore it. Then as soon as she begins doing something more constructive and appropriate, attend to it, describing her actions with emotion.

When you first begin using attends, you should be very descriptive. For instance, you could say, "You're talking with your 'inside' voice," or "You're sharing with Mommy, and she really likes it when you do that." As long as you're attending to okay behavior and ignoring not-okay behavior, the more description the better. Some children may ask, "Why are you doing that?" You can respond by saying, "I just like paying attention to what you're doing."

Praise is another powerful form of positive attention and is a natural extension of attends. As a parent, you want to change what you're looking for. With praise, you seek out opportunities to catch your child behaving well—not only during banking time sessions but also throughout the day. This isn't as easy as it sounds. Many times parents of defiant kids are conditioned to expect misbehavior. In fact, they get to the point where they only notice their child's poor behavior, and attend to it with criticism and complaints. Many parents don't realize they're doing this—particularly parents who tend to overcontrol their kids.

If you have a defiant child, take some time to reflect on whether you're paying attention to the good as well as the bad. If you've been consumed with criticizing and complaining, it'll take some work to change your perspective. But once you're finally able to recognize your child's okay behavior, you'll find that praise can be your most powerful parenting tool.

How to Use Praise

When we talk to parents about praising their kids, many of them say, "We try to praise our child all the time, but it doesn't really help." But usually, when we look a little more closely at how they praise their kids, it's easy to see why it doesn't work.

There are six key principles for making praise effective:

Be specific.

When you praise your child, be sure to connect it to something specific he has done. For example, if he's playing nicely with his toys, say something like, "Brandon, I really like how you're playing so quietly all by yourself. You're being such a big boy!" By being specific, your child can better understand how his behavior affects you. Avoid making comments like, "Brandon, you're being so good. Mommy is really proud of you." This doesn't explain what he's doing that makes you happy, and it's less likely to encourage his quiet, self-directed playtime.

Be immediate.

When you catch your child behaving well, shell out the praise promptly. The quicker the praise, the stronger it will be.

COMBINE VERBAL PRAISE WITH PHYSICAL TOUCH.

There are times when a pat on the back, a tousle of the hair, or a big hug can make your verbal praise more powerful and meaningful. The key is to discover what type of physical touch your child seems to enjoy the most. My (Gary's) son, Jacob, for example, doesn't like being hugged—especially in public. But he really likes it when I cup my hand and rub the back of his head, right by the hairline of his buzzed-cut head. If your kids don't like any kind of physical touch, look for other ways to reinforce your praise.

SEARCH FOR OPPORTUNITIES TO PRAISE.

Here, the goal is to sharpen your awareness of when your child is even the tiniest bit compliant and praise and attend her. Instead of seeking out misbehavior, you want to catch her behaving appropriately. For example, if your daughter has trouble sitting quietly at the table during meals, try to find her sitting still—even for just a second—and praise her: "Megan, I really like the way you're sitting quietly like a big girl, not bouncing around. And you're also using your spoon instead of your hands . . . that's great!"

USE FADING.

There are two ways to use positive reinforcement. If you want your kids to repeat new behavior, then provide praise and positive attention, and usually you'll see that behavior learned and repeated. As your kids display the behavior more frequently, you praise them less frequently: instead of praising them every time, praise them every third or fourth time, and then every fifth or sixth time. This technique, called *fading*, helps ensure the behavior will continue.

USE IGNORING.

Ignoring can be one of the most powerful ways you can help your child eliminate some of her most annoying behaviors, such as whining, tattling, complaining, and fighting. Unfortunately, when you first begin to use ignoring, the target behavior will increase. For example, many parents we work with want to target whining. When they start ignoring this behavior, their kids frequently turn it up, hoping to get a response. But if you're persistent and you follow these principles, your kids will eventually give up.

How long does it take to see improvement? It depends on how severe the behavior is, and how long you've been entrenched in the old methods of attending to your child. Remember, though, it will eventually get better.

IDENTIFY SPECIFIC NOT-OKAY BEHAVIORS YOU WANT TO ELIMINATE.

Ignoring works best on attention-seeking behavior like interrupting, eye rolling, tongue clicking, and temper tantrums. It's not the right tactic for more serious problems, especially those that are potentially harmful to others, your child, or to property.

BE ACTIVE AND INTENTIONAL.

Ignoring is not a passive behavior. In order for it to be effective, you must stick with it—no matter how much you might want to correct your child's behavior at first. This is crucial, because your kid is going to test your determination.

Intentional ignoring involves four elements:

- No eye contact or watching. When your son starts clicking his tongue, turn away at least ninty degrees and avoid eye contact. This is important because your facial expression—sometimes even the simple act of watching—can reinforce his behavior.

- No talking. This is not a time for preaching, teaching, or scolding. Simply refuse to talk with your child. We teach parents to talk to someone else to clarify why they are ignoring their child. For example, you're talking on the phone and your child is calling you: "Mom . . . Mom . . . MOOOOOOM!" You might say to the person on the line, "My daughter is trying to interrupt me while I'm talking on the phone, and I'm ignoring her." If no one else is around, you might say out loud, "Hannah is trying to get my attention by acting silly, but I'm ignoring her until she stops."

- No touching. Often when kids realize they're being ignored, they'll want to be touched and held, even trying to crawl into their mom or dad's lap. So we encourage parents to stand up while ignoring. If your child wraps himself around your ankles—which really does happen—wait it out but do not pick him up.

- No emotion. This may be the most difficult part of ignoring. Kids can push our emotion buttons like Mozart could play the piano! But keep in mind that your response will give them a rush of endorphins. They may not like what you say or do, but they become addicted to the emotional response.

BEGIN IGNORING AS SOON AS NOT-OKAY BEHAVIOR BEGINS.

Don't wait. As soon as you see attention-seeking behavior, actively ignore it. If you first attend to it by scolding—"Cut that out! Why do you have to do that?"—or threatening—"You'd better stop that or . . ."—you won't be nearly as effective.

STOP IGNORING SOON AFTER NOT-OKAY BEHAVIOR ENDS.

We usually tell parents to wait about ten to fifteen seconds and then start looking for okay behavior to praise.

COMBINE IGNORING WITH PRAISE.

Praise and ignoring are much more powerful when you combine them, because you remove the attention that feeds your child's negative behavior and pay attention to more appropriate actions. By doing this, you can retrain your mind, and perhaps more importantly, you learn a new way to relate to your child.

Reversing your mindset can help you become less angry and resentful toward your child. It can also change the way he feels about you. When you combine ignoring and praise, he'll enjoy trying to do things that you approve of. Unlike before, he believes you will notice!

Most of the parents we counsel find that these skills play a crucial role in transforming their kids' behavior—and in the process, improve their confidence. Using attention strategically won't eliminate all their behavior problems, but it will reduce the annoying, irritating, attention-seeking behaviors that can drive us nuts.

TEACHING AND DISCIPLINE

What did your son or daughter learn from you today? Whether you were at home or the office, you taught something to your child—we guarantee it. Just as your kids need time for play and open expression, they also need your teaching and discipline. In fact, God requires it. For instance, God selected Abraham, one of the Bible's greatest father figures, to instill a legacy of godliness in the children of Israel: "For I have chosen him, so that he will direct his children and his household after him to keep the way of the LORD by doing what is right and just, so that the LORD will bring about for Abraham what he has promised him" (Genesis 18:19).

Your children will probably ask you "why?" about a million times between the ages of one and eighteen. Sure, it can be irritating. But try not to take their questioning for granted.

Each time your child asks "why?" you have the opportunity to teach him an important life lesson. The Bible speaks to the significance of such wisdom and correction, saying, "For these commands are a lamp, this teaching is a light, and the corrections of discipline are the way to life" (Proverbs 6:23).

We need to step up to the plate and teach our kids godly wisdom and basic morality—right from wrong. The truth may be obvious to us, but it isn't to our kids, especially since many schools today teach children relativism and watered-down "situational" ethics that are not ethical at all. For Christians, the Bible is the only infallible guide for teaching morality. And teaching our kids God's truth does make a difference! Studies show that children who are raised without objective standards of truth are:

48 percent more likely to cheat on an exam

2 times more likely to get drunk

3 times more likely to use illegal drugs

6 times more likely to attempt suicide[2]

The following chart is a checklist you can use to discuss biblical principles of right and wrong in a modern context. You and your child can fill out separate copies or develop your own chart and then discuss how your answers differ.

Of course, moral guidance consists of more than checking boxes and having good conversations with our kids—it's also about living out what we're trying to teach them. For example, when you ask your daughter to answer the door and tell the Girl Scout selling cookies that you're not home, or when you answer the phone and tell a telemarketer he has the wrong number, you're teaching your child that it's okay to bear false witness—to

Always	Maybe	Never	Is it okay to . . .
			SOCIAL
			Tell a parent she has a beautiful baby when she doesn't?
			Tease or scare others?
			Cheat at cards or videogames?
			Let a friend copy your homework?
			Ride in a car with a friend who speeds?
			RELIGION
			Go to a non-Christian place of worship?
			Participate in Halloween?
			PERSONAL
			Try smoking or drugs?
			Have a beer at a party?
			Shave your head?
			Get a tattoo?
			Swear?
			Watch an R-rated movie?
			Kiss a boyfriend/girlfriend?

lie if it's convenient. And no matter how many talks you have with her about the importance of honesty, she will never unlearn what you've already taught her.

If we want to foster good behavior and a strong conscience in our kids, we must ensure we're teaching them Christian values and morals through both our words and actions—not leaving ethical education up to school, prime-time TV, or the kid next door. We need to give our kids a solid foundation of biblical values, first introducing them to what we believe and then allowing them to form their own opinions and attitudes. With this foundation of truth, our discipline will be most effective.

WHAT IS DISCIPLINE?

Discipline is not punishment. It is the process of teaching our kids right from wrong by setting limits, making those limits clear, and enforcing them. As parents, we are not punishing wrong behavior when we discipline; we're shaping character. We are not simply setting limits; we're also teaching our kids how to distinguish right from wrong. The dictionary defines the word *discipline* as, "Training expected to produce a specific character or pattern of behavior, especially training that produces moral or mental improvement."[3] In contrast, *punishment* is defined as, "A penalty imposed for wrongdoing. Or rough handling; mistreatment: *These old skis have taken a lot of punishment over the years.*"[4]

If you're confused by the difference between discipline and punishment, remember that your goal as a parent is to teach your child "self-discipline," not "self-punishment." Dr. James

Dobson writes that parents should unabashedly use discipline—for the good of their children.⁵ If correction is done in a loving way—one that does not overcontrol, overindulge, or overprotect—discipline will help you to raise content, God-centered kids.

In order to best discipline your kids, it's helpful to remember some key principles:

CREATE AN ENVIRONMENT FOR MORAL GROWTH.

The book of Genesis tells us that when Lot and his wife moved to Sodom and Gomorrah, they were unable to grow spiritually. Eventually God led them from that immoral city. Just as God protected Lot's family, so must we protect our own. It's up to us as parents to make sure our kids live in a safe, moral environment where they can thrive spiritually, physically, and emotionally. For instance, if you often leave your teenagers unsupervised—a time in which they are still developing their own convictions—you shouldn't be surprised when they succumb to peer pressure. Environment can be everything. Scripture says that Samuel, who became a prophet, "grew up in the presence of the LORD" (1 Samuel 2:21). He even slept next to the ark of God in the temple (see 1 Samuel 3:3). Do your best to give your children the same opportunity for spiritual growth.

ESTABLISH CLEAR RULES AND LIMITS.

Kids need to understand clearly what is and what is not acceptable before they can be expected to stay within those limits.

When kids are punished or corrected for doing something they didn't even know was wrong, they get angry and discouraged. It's hard enough for them to follow definite rules, let alone vague ones.

TEACH YOUR CHILD THE REASONS BEHIND YOUR RULES.

When you tell your child what to do without giving her any explanation other than "because I said so"—something over-controlling parents often do—she will soon resent you for it. If you don't explain why, she won't really learn anything and will forget your rules as soon as you leave the scene. But if you teach her the biblical reasons behind your rules, she will carry with them with her!

DISCERN BETWEEN INTENTIONAL DEFIANCE AND CHILDISH IRRESPONSIBILITY.

This is perhaps the most important guideline for good discipline: children should be corrected only for willful defiance, not childhood irresponsibility. Paul Meier writes, "At about eight or nine months of age parents may begin saying 'no' as they pull the baby away from forbidden objects. This will need to be repeated many times for most children. After ten or fifteen times of saying 'no' and pulling away the child, some parents may wonder if they have a slow learner on their hands, but this is simply the normal way children learn at this age."[6] With that in mind, pair your expectations and correction with the age and maturity of your child.

There's a difference between purposely breaking a rule and irresponsibly making an error that violates a rule. For example, if Joey tripped and spilled his blue Gatorade on the white carpet while carrying his dishes to the kitchen, or if seven-year-old Sophie left her skates outside in the rain because she was late for church, that would be childish irresponsibility.

But sometimes it's not always clear. If Scott broke his curfew, was it because he willfully decided not to pay attention to the time (defiance), because he chose to be late (defiance), or because he forgot to wear a watch to the youth group's bowling party? The latter is an example of childish irresponsibility and is absolutely normal as kids "learn" discipline. Often it can be a tough job to discern when a child is willfully disobeying or simply making mistakes.

It takes time to learn discipline. Encourage your children to try and try again, and don't punish them for normal developmental accidents. Sometimes breaking curfew really is an accident.

AVOID MAKING IMPOSSIBLE DEMANDS.

Make sure you're establishing rules and limits your child can follow. Also, keep in mind that what is impossible for one child may be no big deal for another and set limits—and discipline—accordingly.

One frustrated parent of a hyperactive six-year-old girl told us, "My son can follow directions, but my daughter just won't listen to me! I clean the house all day, so I tell her before she leaves for school, 'When you get home, come in through the garage and take off your boots, winter coat, and backpack before you step into the house.' And every day she rushes in through the front door, boots and all!" The girl wasn't being defiant; she was just excited to be home, and in her excitement, she forgot the rules—until she saw her angry mother! Instead of constantly doling out correction, this mother needed to do a little problem solving with her daughter. Perhaps there needed to be a small area next to the front door where a little disorder could be tolerated so that the girl could remain, over the years, excited to come home.

TEACH VIRTUES THAT STRENGTHEN AND GUIDE BEHAVIOR.

Effective discipline is more than just correcting your child when he's wrong. It's also being proactive and teaching your child skills to help him handle potentially disastrous situations. For example, schools try and teach kids to say no to drugs at an age before they're likely to be offered them. As parents, we can reinforce the school's teaching and take it a step further—teaching our kids to obey the law, to respect their bodies as a temple of the Holy Spirit, and to follow Christian virtues that are incompatible with drug use.

There are many virtues you can teach your children, and when you do, your kids will learn to set their own limits and rules—the final test of true discipline.

LET LOVE GUIDE YOU.

Correction is very taxing to the parent-child relationship. Make sure you have enough deposits into your child's emotional bank account when you discipline, and don't overdraw the account by emphasizing correction over relationship. Remember, it's your relationship with your child, not the correction that truly promotes change. If your motivation is to raise healthy, strong kids in love, using God's love and biblical principles as a guide, you will do well!

Discipline Tips:

- Correct willful defiance, not juvenile carelessness or irresponsibility.

- Discipline children for what they do, not for how they feel.

- When confronting a problem, begin by deciding what you want to accomplish, and how your corrections will help—not hurt—your child.

- Respond—don't react.

- Use your kids' misbehavior to teach them. Always explain calmly why their behavior was inappropriate and unacceptable.

- Not all violations need a strict consequence. It's important to show grace and mercy.

- Remember, discipline is about correction and instruction, not punishment!

ENFORCING CORRECTION

Kids need to know that their parents will administer correction with consistency, tenacity, grace, and firmness. They should also understand that the level of their correction reflects the severity of their crime, not their mom or dad's mood or temper.

No parent likes to enforce correction when the rules are willfully defied, but it's an important part of the discipline process.

We like to think of this rod as that of the ever-present shepherd's rod, used to prod the wayward sheep away from danger and to direct them.

The Bible has a lot to say about the importance of correction too:

"He who spares the rod hates his son, but he who loves him is careful to discipline him" (Proverbs 13:24).

"No discipline seems pleasant at the time, but painful. Later on, however, it produces a harvest of righteousness and peace for those who have been trained by it" (Hebrews 12:11).

"Blessed is the man whom God corrects; so do not despise the discipline of the Almighty" (Job 5:17).

"Discipline your son, and he will give you peace; he will bring delight to your soul" (Proverbs 29:17).

To make sure the correction is appropriate for the offense, we provide four levels of enforcement. As you read, keep in mind that some children are very sensitive to correction—it takes very little to get the point across—while others need more strict discipline. Lecturing alone (level one) may work wonders for your daughter, but your son may need to have his privileges revoked as well (level three).

With each level of correction, be decisive and respond with authority. Correct your child immediately. When you act quickly, he will associate his defiance with your correction. Then once the correction takes place, get beyond it. Move on with your relationship and life with your child.

LEVEL 1: LECTURING

Words can be powerful: God created the world with words (see Genesis 1). They can also be terrifying: Jesus cursed a fruitless fig tree, and it withered and died (Matthew 21:19).

Similarly, the "roar" of a parent is often enough to correct a child for misbehavior and get her to reform. But when you lecture, don't send the message to your child that she is "no good." Simply communicate to her that she's made a mistake. Instead of criticizing her character, correct her behavior, saying, "You're not minding your manners, young lady! Use your napkin." You can also warn her that she must shape up or the correction will become more severe.

LEVEL 2: TIME-OUT

Used properly, brief time-outs can help children stop inappropriate behavior. They can also provide kids the opportunity to calm down and recenter their emotions.

Time-outs can also be used inappropriately, though. Sometimes parents put their kids in hefty time-outs to get even with them for their bad behavior, or they punish their kids with an in-room prison sentence because they want them out of their hair for a long time. But what this does is simply give kids time to sit in their rooms and plot how to get back at their parents!

When you put your child in time-out, take into consideration the amount of time that is appropriate for his age. Some experts recommend one minute for every year of age, but we believe it really depends on the circumstances. Rather than simply accounting for age, you should also ask, "How much time does my child need to calm down and recenter his emotions?" Also, time-outs do not mean that parents get a break. Whenever my (Tim) son, Zach, was sent to his room for time-out, his mother or I would go with him, keeping the bond strong even during correction.

LEVEL 3: REMOVING PRIVILEGES

When Nick refused to turn his stereo down after several requests, his parents simply removed it from his room, reminding him that he knew beforehand the consequence of his defiance. They also told him he would lose the privilege for twenty-four hours.

The good thing about this type of correction is that as soon as the stereo is gone, the parent-child tension dissolves and Nick and his parents can work together to decide what they'll do for entertainment that day. It often helps the disciplinary process when parents suffer the same punishment they impose on their children. If Julia loses TV privileges, then the whole family does too. This communicates to children that you're in the trenches with them.

LEVEL 4: SPANKING

There is never a place for slapping, hitting, and striking a child. Christian psychiatrist Paul Meier warns parents, "We do not believe in child abuse of any form. Punishment by striking a child is dangerous for some parents whose anger can make them hit harder than they intended."[7] In contrast, spanking consists of one or two swats applied to the child's bottom with a paddle of some sort—done firmly enough to be felt, but softly enough to ensure you don't leave a mark.

Not all children need this correction either. If you've never had to spank your child, it may simply be that he responds well to the other three levels of correction. If your child does need this level of correction, we recommend reserving swats for very serious offenses, and only for instances where he has repeatedly and willfully defied you.

According to Dr. James Dobson, physical correction should not be used with a child younger than fifteen months of age, and even then, the proper correction is a slap on the hand. The safest guideline is that physical correction can be used between seventeen months and six years of age. Between ages six and nine, spanking should be used sparingly. We do not recommend physical correction after kids are nine years old, because at that time it seems to lose its therapeutic power, and there's more risk of causing emotional harm.

We also recommend that you use a light paddle to provide two to three swats on the rear end, rather than your hand. This is not flogging your kid into submission, but using a small amount of pain as correction. Hitting should never be so hard as to leave a mark. You know the cliché where the parent says, "This will hurt me more than it hurts you"? That is really how it should be.

Also, never discipline when you're angry. This sends the message to your child that it's okay to swat people when they bother you. First calm down and talk to your child about what his correction is and why he is receiving it. Remember, if he's at level 4 correction, he has had plenty of warnings along the way!

Finally, keep in mind that some kids actually get worse with spankings, even though their behavior is out of control, angry, defiant, and even aggressive. It seems that the more parents use this technique, the worse their child becomes. If this is the case, and many of the other suggestions we have offered are not helping, we encourage you to seek professional consultation. These kids may have such significant emotional and behavior problems that they have trouble learning from their mistakes and managing their strong, negative, hostile feelings.

Remember, discipline is about maintaining a strong bond with your kids while teaching them important life lessons! It bears repeating: as a parent, your ability to discipline your children relates directly to the level of relationship you have with them.

Even in the midst of discipline, your children should feel fully loved. Our goal is to parent like God, with the perfect balance of discipline and love. Proper discipline is a form of love, as the Bible says in Proverbs 3:12 "because the LORD disciplines those he loves, as a father the son he delights in." Yet our children should have complete assurance that we love them with a "lavish" love as it says in 1 John 3:1 "How great is the love the Father has lavished on us, that we should be called children of God! And that is what we are!"

chapter fourteen

EXTRA-EFFORT KIDS

WITH ANTHONY J. CENTORE, PH.D.

There was a man who had two sons. The younger one said to his father,
"Father, give me my share of the estate."
So he divided his property between them.

Not long after that, the younger son got together
all he had, set off for a distant country and there squandered
his wealth in wild living.

Luke 15:11–13

𝒯om and Krista were in the checkout line at the grocery store when they heard some commotion one aisle over. A preschool-age boy had thrown himself on the floor and was holding on to the bottom of a rack of candy. "I want candy! I'm not letting go until you give me some!" he yelled. His flustered mom—who also had a baby seated in the cart—turned red and tried unsuccessfully to pry her son off the floor.

"Stop it, Zach!" she hissed, trying to unhinge his fingers. "I mean it!"

"No!"

She shot an apologetic look at the checkout clerk and the line of people that had begun to snake behind her. Then she looked at her son again. He stared defiantly back at her.

"Fine!" she said with resignation. "Just this once."

After the woman left, Krista and Tom—who incidentally had well-mannered children—turned and gave each other knowing looks. Tom whispered, "Our kids would never act that way because they know we wouldn't put up with that kind of behavior."

Krista nodded and rolled her eyes.

Like many parents might, Tom and Krista made several assumptions:

- The mother dealing with the temper tantrum is an incompetent parent.

- The child is throwing a temper tantrum because he thinks he can get away with it.

- The mother can't discipline her son and she lets him walk all over her.

Maybe you're like Tom and Krista. You see unmanageable children in public and decide their parents should be forced to attend some sort of remedial parenting class, without knowing the history or the facts about the situation. Or, more likely, maybe you can relate to that struggling mother. You've tried many different tactics to be a good and loving parent, but you just can't seem to get your children under control.

Maybe you've felt the judgmental stares of your neighbors, or gotten unsolicited parenting advice on how to make your kid behave. Maybe you've even taken that advice and wished in the end that you'd done nothing at all!

Parenting a difficult child requires not only that you try to understand her needs but also that you look at your own shortcomings. Remember, if you tend to overcontrol, overprotect, or overindulge, it will make parenting all the more difficult. As counselors, we see parents every day who are just like you, struggling to raise a challenging child with very little support and even less solid guidance. We know what you're feeling, and we want to encourage you not to give up. There are practical steps you can take to improve your relationship with your child.

DOES YOUR CHILD HAVE A BEHAVIOR PROBLEM?

How do you feel about your child's behavior? Like their kids, all parents have different tolerance levels. You may be flexible and easygoing about your child's misconduct and have gotten complaints from your kid's teachers or daycare workers. Or you may be constantly critical while other adults consider your child a likeable kid. To help determine if a problem really exists, use the behavior-rating scale on the next page to objectively rate your child's actions.

If you checked "Often" or "Very Often" less than four times, then your child's behavior, although frustrating, falls within a normal range. But if you have checked four or more and these

DEFIANT BEHAVIOR	Never	Sometimes	Often	Very Often
Loses temper				
Argues with adults				
Actively defies or refuses to comply with adults' requests				
Deliberately annoys people				
Blames others for his or her mistakes and misbehavior				
Touchy or easily annoyed by others				
Angry and resentful				
Spiteful and vindictive				

problems have been around for at least six months, it's likely that your child has a legitimate, diagnosable behavior problem.

Of course, if you have an adolescent and he is hyper, depressed, anxious, or angry, he may just be going through a phase. Adolescents experience all kinds of physical, mental, and social changes. They get moody because of hormones, rebel because they long for freedom, and push the boundaries as they explore higher levels of abstract thought. All this change can be considered a phase and is absolutely normal. But if you frequently feel overwhelmed with frustration and worry, it's a good sign that your child is no longer in just a phase, but is experiencing a real behavior problem.

The Strong-Willed Child

Author and speaker Cynthia Ulrich Tobias said it well when she described a power struggle with her strong-willed son:

> "Michael Tobias, you need to pick those toys up and put them in the basket now!" Even as I heard myself issue the order to my four-year-old, I realized I was in trouble. I sometimes forget that I am dealing with a child who is just as strong-willed as I am, and barking out orders has never been an effective means of communicating with me. But I had already climbed out on my limb, and I was not about to come back.
>
> Noting that Mike was making no move to clean up, I moved a little further out on the limb. "Mike, if I have to pick up those toys, I am going to give them to some other kids." He shrugged. "Give them to some other kids," he said. I could not hide my surprise. Some of those toys were among his favorites. But he had just climbed out on his limb, too. Without another word, I scooped up the toys and took them to the garage. Later in the week, I gave the toys to a ministry at our church. Six months later, he had never once asked for any of those toys. He knew that he had called my bluff, and he was fully prepared to accept the consequences.[1]

From birth to adulthood, strong-willed kids challenge their parents. What's more, parents of these children know that the discipline strategies that might work with other kids don't have the same effect on theirs. However, the strong-willed child is often misunderstood. Even though many people think that a strong will denotes defiance and rebellion, "strong-willed" is defined by the Princeton University WordNet dictionary as "having a determined will." We believe firmly that determination is not a negative trait!

When parents bring out the best in a strong-willed child they discover incredible strength and potential within her. Strong-willed children are born leaders, and they want to be treated with courtesy and respect. Their attitudes reference both the Emancipation Proclamation (which ended slavery) and the Bill of Rights. Similarly, they don't always have trouble with authority itself, but sometimes they do need help learning to live within limits set by persons with authority over them.

There are ways to ease these lessons. For example, instead of telling your child "Pick up those toys right now," you'll find better results by saying, "I know you like having your toys spread out, but company is coming over soon and they need to be put away." Instead of declaring "No Playstation before school," try saying "I know you want to play Playstation, but the bus will be here soon and you still need to get your shoes and coat on." A friendly and respectful tone does not indicate weakness on your part. Your rules remain intact and you maintain all your authority as a parent. At the same time, your child feels that her feelings matter and she learns that living under authority is not so bad.[2]

Strong-willed kids don't like being controlled, and they know intuitively that they always have the choice to obey, or not. When parents, teachers, coaches or anyone barks orders such as, "You will . . . ," "You must . . ." or even "because I said so," these children rebel with determined disobedience. Even when the consequences are unpleasant, to the strong-willed kid, punishment is better than enslavement. When we enforce the rules as parents, we need to realize that our kids can never really be forced to do anything. Even with all our parental authority, it is simply impossible to make Deborah eat her dinner if she doesn't want to. As we have said earlier, the quality of our relationship with our children determines the effectiveness of our discipline. When we communicate to our strong-willed kids that we love and respect them, obedience becomes much less of a battle. Deborah will think to herself. "I don't want to eat this, but mom really wants me to. I know she cares about me and wants what's best for me. I guess I can choose to finish my dinner anyway."

Amazingly, this same trait of having a strong will, while viewed with derision in childhood, is honored and valued in adulthood! Why then, would we ever want to try and break the will of our kids? Teach the child empathy, compassion, love, cooperation, self-respect, respect for others, how to accept and how to make rules and requests. With these skills, the strong-willed child will go far!

Attention Deficit Hyperactivity Disorder (ADHD)

Recently, Jen brought her fourteen-year-old daughter, Sawyer, to counseling. Sawyer's grades had been falling—over the course of the school year, her A's had turned into D's and even F's. Her teachers were complaining that she wasn't paying attention in class, instead staring blankly at the wrong page of her textbook. Moreover, she had turned into a loner, spending long hours in her bedroom doing nothing at all, avoiding her few friends.

"She used to be so happy and likeable," Jen lamented. "I thought she was just going through an early teen phase!"

"What happened?" we asked.

Jen shook her head in frustration. "She just got more and more moody!"

After several months, she took Sawyer to their family doctor, who first thought she was suffering from depression, then sleep deprivation, then an iron deficiency. None was the case. In fact, it seemed like no matter what her parents did, Sawyer continued her downward spiral.

"I try to help her. I say, 'Sawyer, what is it? What's wrong?'" Jen told us. "But she tunes me out. It's like she's trying to ignore me!"

Sawyer wasn't intentionally ignoring her mother—she had Attention Deficit Hyperactivity Disorder (ADHD). ADHD is one of the most common childhood disorders. The American Psychiatric Association estimates that between 3 and 7 percent of children suffer from ADHD, and many other children who don't actually qualify for the diagnosis still struggle with significant symptoms.[3]

Kids with ADHD are chronically inattentive, hyperactive, or both—so much so that their daily lives are disrupted. They have trouble paying attention in class, doing their homework, finishing their chores, and adjusting their behavior to meet the demands of a situation. As a result, they struggle in their friendships, family relationships, and school performance.

There are three types of ADHD:[4]

THE INATTENTIVE TYPE

Kids with ADHD have no problem paying attention to things they find exciting and enjoyable, like their video games or favorite cartoons. It's the things that seem boring and unnecessary that they struggle to pay attention to, like memorizing their multiplication tables, reading their assignments, or listening to their mom or dad's lectures.

Other characteristics of inattentive kids include:

- Lack of organization
- Difficulty finishing tasks
- Lack of attention to detail
- Tendency to get distracted
- Withdrawn or shy behavior
- Difficulty with social conversations

THE HYPERACTIVE—IMPULSIVE TYPE

Overactivity has more to do with the situation than the activity level. For example, kids with ADHD are not necessarily more active than their peers on the playground. They just can't adjust their behavior to the situation. For instance, when they come in from recess, they have trouble calming down. They can't sit still, and they disrupt the rest of their classmates with their loud voices and boisterous activity.

They also have difficulty delaying gratification. Renowned ADHD expert Russell Barkely describes these kids as being "creatures of the moment." They will spend all their allowance each week rather than save up for something nice.

Hyperactive-impulsive kids also display:

- Frequent fidgeting
- Over-talkativeness
- Difficulty sitting or standing still
- Overactivity (running, jumping, climbing)
- Impulsiveness
- Restlessness
- Aggressive behavior
- Inappropriate social behavior (such as grabbing things and speaking out of turn)

COMBINED TYPE

These ADHD kids don't tend toward one category or the other. They can be equally inattentive and hyperactive-impulsive.

Left untreated, ADHD can affect a child's growth and development. Kids with ADHD often are not involved in after-school or recreational activities. Their parents are half as likely to say that their ADHD kids have a lot of good friends, and more than twice as likely to report that their children are picked on at school or have trouble getting along with their peers. These social problems put children at risk for anxiety, behavior and mood disorders, substance abuse, and teen delinquency.[5]

Many children with ADHD also develop other behavioral problems, such as angry defiance. Their ADHD symptoms can create so many problems with adults that they develop anger, resentment, and disrespect toward authority.

Fortunately, there are both medical treatments and behavioral steps that can help kids with ADHD. Though they are not a cure for the disorder, these steps—outlined later in the chapter—can greatly improve your relationship with your child, fostering a supportive environment where she can grow and reach her God-given potential.

THE OPPOSITIONAL DEFIANT CHILD

Carrie was a stay-at-home mom who, with her husband David, had been trying her best to raise her four-year-old son, Joshua. Since birth, Joshua had been fussy, angry, frustrated, and temperamental, defying even the most innocuous commands.

"I don't know what I'm doing wrong!" Carrie said, wiping tears from her eyes. "And we're not horrible parents. We really aren't. We've tried everything, and nothing helps. He just acts the way he acts."

David nodded, then threw his hands in the air. "I really don't understand. He has two parents who are there for him, parents who love him, and he's still such a tyrant."

Carrie and David had tried many things to "fix" Joshua. They had met with their pastor, who recommended prayer; a counselor, who suggested strict discipline programs; and the family doctor, who put Joshua on medication—all to no avail.

After seeing Joshua for several weeks, we diagnosed him with a condition known as Oppositional Defiant Disorder (ODD). Children with ODD have trouble understanding their complicated emotions and how their behavior can be disruptive, hurtful, and irritating. Like many children, they struggle to control their feelings—even when their parents follow emotion coaching. When children have this disability, the typical strategies used to train kids to handle emotional challenges don't work. Tragically, children with this disorder are rarely calm, content, or at peace. This makes the people around them frustrated, worried, and downright miserable!

Shelia, the mother of a tyrannical nine-year-old named Justin, broke down in our office as she described her son's behavior. "I dread seeing his bus come down the road in the afternoon. I have to prepare myself for the exhausting battles that will start as soon as he steps into the house. And then I feel guilty for feeling such resentment toward him. Am I a terrible mom? I'm so far beyond my wits end, I've forgotten what rational thought feels like!"

Oppositional defiance hinges on three main problem areas:

DEFIANCE

When kids turn two, they discover that what they want and what you want may not match. They also express their individuality with gusto—by disagreeing, throwing tantrums, and saying "no!" But with ODD children, the resistance, stubbornness, and defiance are even more extreme. When these kids challenge authority, they're not saying, "I'm different from you," but "I'm really angry at you and I want to make you miserable!"

ODD children are angry, and their mission is to make you angry. As one exasperated mom told us, "My daughter has a special way of getting under my skin and making my blood boil." Some of these kids may see the frustration they are causing their parents and not even care. Others may actually enjoy making others angry and feel justified in doing so. One eleven-year old girl told us, "My parents deserve what they get from me!"

ANGER AND IRRITABILITY

ODD kids are irritable; the slightest thing can set them off. To try to keep their kids happy, some parents of ODD children overindulge them. But even that doesn't work for very long. If they get their way, they *might* be okay for a while, but even gifts and money aren't enough to keep them happy.

Unlike anxious children who pull away from their world when they get upset, these defiant children try to control their world. They use violence and irritability to manage their life and relationships. They don't trust others, especially adults, to make decisions for them. As a result, they want to take charge—of the entire family. Of course, this take-charge approach doesn't go over well.

Many ODD children are also very emotionally and physically sensitive. Leading child psychiatrist Stanley Greenspan notes that the defiant child feels that her protection from the world is very thin: sound, sight, taste, smell, touch, or any of the senses that are pleasant to others may irritate and overwhelm her. Parents often remark that their ODD child will complain about the tag on the back of her shirt or that her pants don't fit right. "Anything out of the ordinary puts her in crisis mode," said one mother about her nine-year-old daughter.

NEGATIVITY

ODD kids are famous for their negativity. They often see even good things that would enthuse most people as irritations. One parent complained, "When we want to do something fun—go to a movie or out for dinner—Isaiah puts up the biggest stink. So we just stay home. The other children resent him for it." It's easy for parents to resent their ODD children, too, when they resist things like eating at their favorite restaurant or playing their favorite board game.

On the other hand, if they want to do something and you don't, prepare to be prodded, begged, and shown a level of pleading seen only on death row. If you take a stand, these kids may hit the floor in a full-blown temper tantrum or pout and sulk for several hours.

THERE IS HOPE

If any of these profiles describe your child, remember this: your kid is not acting up because he *wants* to be bad. It requires a great deal of self-control to follow other people's rules and demands—especially if he, like many extra-effort kids, struggles with self-control.

And there is hope. After counseling countless families, we've come up with some biblically based principles in addition to well-researched methods for changing children's behavior. What's fascinating is that the biblical principles are clearly supported by research in developmental psychology and child therapy. And many of the methods are no different from parenting well-adjusted, less-defiant children. It is the following emotion-laden back-and-forth exchanges between parents and children that help kids develop and grow in the ways we described earlier in this book. We've listed several of them here:

LEARN TO ACCEPT YOUR CHILD.

Some parents—especially those who overcontrol—come to us for help with their kids but don't want to accept that their children have different temperaments, dreams, skills, and weaknesses. Many will ask for help with a behavior problem, but almost without exception, they're actually seeking to change the child's uniqueness and temperament. These parents will say, "Help me get rid of my child's stubbornness!" rather than, "Help me teach my child how to express his anger in a more constructive way."

These parents need to decide at some point whether they are going to accept their child's uniqueness, however challenging it may be, and commit to rebuilding the relationship. We often ask them, "Are you willing to do what is necessary to build a healthy relationship with your child?" Parents don't need to accept defiant behavior, but they do need to accept their kids' unique temperament.

STOP PLAYING THE BLAME GAME.

Mrs. Hathaway was pleased as she surveyed her fifth-grade classroom at the end of the first week of school. All her children were motivated to learn, happy, pleasant, and good listeners—except for Josalyn. Josalyn spent half her time each day looking out the window. She'd take out a sheet of paper and a pencil, but she wouldn't write any notes.

Mrs. Hathaway found this endlessly frustrating. *Look at everyone else in the class,* she told herself. *They pay attention, do their homework, take proper notes, and score well on tests. I can't be held responsible for one lazy, disrespectful child who won't pay attention.*

Most teachers and school systems thought this way for decades. If one of their students had a behavior problem, they would blame it on the child. But today we know more about learning disabilities and attention deficit problems, and we know that Josalyn might not be lazy—she might simply have a different learning style.

The same applies to temperament. Like Josalyn's teacher, parents often blame their kids for being difficult or deficient. But once we make a commitment to build a relationship with our child, we forfeit the right to blame her for being difficult. Some parents may say, "My son is just spoiled!" when the truth is that he has difficult temperament. Another parent might say, "My daughter constantly pouts and acts miserable" when her child has been battling depression due to all the changes at home.

Blaming will make it virtually impossible to improve your relationship with your child. Besides, as parents, we must take complete responsibility for our own behavior. The apostle Paul said, "You, therefore, have no excuse, you who pass judgment on someone else, for at whatever point you judge the other, you are condemning yourself, because you who pass judgment do the same things" (Romans 2:1). We are accountable for what we do—whether we're parenting a child who is defiant or easy. Your child may be "a pain" but that doesn't mean you get to be "a pain" in return.

DECIDE IF THERE ARE ANY CONTRIBUTING FACTORS.

Children who have emotional disabilities or difficult temperaments struggle with basic factors that may have little or no effect on other kids. For instance, they don't do as well with unclear rules or change. Even minor adjustments like temporary schedule changes can upset them, such as when mom or dad work hours of overtime or a new family friend starts spending a lot of time around the house.

Other factors like poor monitoring—paying attention to bad behavior and ignoring good behavior—overcontrolling, or family stress can also affect children with behavioral problems.

SPEND TIME WITH YOUR CHILD AND LET HIM TAKE THE LEAD.

Banking time, a technique first developed by renowned ADHD and ODD expert Russell Barkley, can be extremely effective with children who have behavioral problems. The simple act of setting aside fifteen to twenty minutes every day, letting your child take the lead in play, can restore positive feelings in the relationship. The same principle applies to having conversations with your kids. Create opportunities to chat with your kids, following their lead in the conversation. This helps children with behavioral problems to learn how to interact with adults and become more comfortable sharing things with their parents.

EMPATHIZE AND PROBLEM-SOLVE.

Empathy has two parts: first understanding how your child feels and then communicating that understanding to him. The goal is to seek to understand before being understood. It's important for parents to empathize, especially with children who have behavioral problems, and particularly when they're upset. Why? Empathy can serve two purposes—strengthening the relationship, and helping children understand how and why they feel the way they do. When kids are empathetic, they develop self-control and more social behavior.

Many parents tend to jump to problem solving and ignore empathizing. But problem solving will never be successful if their children don't feel understood. We encourage parents to have problem-solving discussions with their kids on a daily basis, breaking larger problems down into smaller, more manageable ones.

Once the relationship is restored, you might consider following more-structured discipline techniques, such as point programs, removing privileges, and time-outs. But in many cases, once you've empathized with your child you'll find this kind of discipline is unnecessary, even with a difficult child.

REALIZE THAT CLOSE RELATIONSHIPS CAN BE COSTLY.

The apostle Paul wrote about intimacy, saying: "Be devoted to one another in brotherly love. Honor one another above yourselves" (Romans 12:10). "Live in harmony with one another. Do not be proud, but be willing to associate with people of low position" (Romans 12:16). "Let no debt remain outstanding, except the continuing debt to love one another" (Romans 13:8).

As Paul explained, true love comes at a cost. If we want to experience intimacy, we have to deal with the problems that will arise when we get close to another person. Our child may have a much different temperament than we do, or he might be a challenging, defiant kid. The essence of Christian philosophy, however, is that we treat him with kindness, even if he treats us unkindly.

Some parents believe that if they repay disrespect with kindness, they'll be reinforcing their child's bad behavior. That thinking is backward, though! This fire-for-fire mind-set exists nowhere in New Testament scripture, and it certainly doesn't reflect the nature of Christ. God does not repay our sin with equal sin. Instead, when we repent, He forgives us, treating us with the kindness and compassion we don't deserve . . . but desperately need (see Romans 5:8).

Change your mind.

There is a strong connection between how we think, feel, and behave, and the impact our thinking has on our child's feelings and behaviors. Negative thinking patterns can create self-fulfilling prophesies with our kids. For example, thinking that your child is "always" into trouble will lead you to look for misbehavior and ignore good behavior. As a result, your child tells himself, *I can't do anything to please my parents, so why try?* Ironically, this "I don't care" attitude is likely to get him into more trouble with you—which is what you expected from him in the first place!

It is difficult to change your perceptions about a person. Pray that God will help you see your child in a new light. Ask that you will be able to see your child the way God Himself does.

REFLECTING HIS GRACE

When God gives us a difficult child to parent, He also gives us the opportunity to model a Christlike attitude. As parents, we have the ability to reflect God's respect, love, mercy, and grace to children who really need it—in some ways more than we could show to their more-obedient peers. It can be both emotionally and physically taxing to build a relationship with a difficult child. But the benefits are well worth the effort.

Parents, we know that whether you're raising a challenging kid or an easy one, you don't get a lot of affirmation for all the effort you put forth. So we'd like to thank you. And as we tell every parent we counsel, we don't believe there is a trial or situation beyond the reach, love, and care of God (see Romans 8:39). We've seen God do wonderful work in a lot of parents and children. So look to Him with a spirit of expectation. He will make a way for you!

If the road has been long and difficult and you are not seeing significant changes, seek out your pastor, a spiritual friend, or a professional Christian counselor. You can also find more helpful resources and even a listing of professional counselors in your area through the American Association of Christian Counselors Web site (AACC.net).

A FINAL WORD . . .

The Bible says children are a heritage from the Lord, a special gift. They are on loan from God, given to us for only a season. As parents, our primary, God-given responsibility is to help our kids become more like Him. And we can do that when we give our kids a healthy, godly love.

So tonight when you tuck your daughter in bed, or gaze at that young man across the dinner table, be sure to take a second look. Touch her face as she sleeps. Kiss his forehead. Squeeze her hand. Join us in praying, "Father, the day is coming when my kids will be grown up and gone. Please give me the wisdom and strength to love my kids as You love me. Thank You for loving me with an everlasting and perfect love. In Jesus' name, amen."

And always remember, you can never love them too much.

NOTES

CHAPTER ONE: CAN YOU REALLY LOVE YOUR KIDS TOO MUCH?

1. D. Burns, "It's All Your Fault" (workshop on cognitive interpersonal therapy for relationship disturbances).

2. G. W. Bush, remarks to the fourth national summit on fatherhood, Ticonderoga Room at the Hyatt Regency Washington on Capitol Hill, June 7, 2001, *Administration of George W. Bush*, 859–61.

3. Estimate of professionals in the field.

4. S. I. Greenspan and Serena Wieder, *The child with Special Needs: Encouraging Intellectual and Emotional Growth* (USA: Da Capo, 1998).

5. *The Wall Street Journal*, 2005.

6. L. Bauman and R. Riche. *The Ten Most Troublesome Teen-Age Problems and How to Solve Them* (Secaucus, NJ: Citadel Press, 1998).

7. D. Blackenhorn, *Fatherless America: Confronting Our Most Urgent Social Problem* (New York: BasicBooks, 1995).

8. Population Reference Bureau. 2000 Census data: Living arrangements profile for United States. *Analysis of Data from the U.S. Census Bureau, for The Annie E. Casey Foundation*, www.aecf.org (accessed May 2005).

9. American Academy of Child and Adolescent Psychiatry, "Teen Suicide," (June 2004) http://www.aacap.org/publications/factsfam/suicide.htm (accessed November 28, 2005).

10. Center for Disease Control, "Federal activities addressing violence in schools,"(2000) http://www.cdc.gov/HealthyYouth/injury/pdf/violenceactivities.pdf (accessed November 3, 2005).

11. J. M. Twenge, K. W. Campbell, C. A. Foster, "Parenthood and Marital Satisfaction: A Meta-Analytic Review," *Journal of Marriage and Family* 65, no. 3, (2003): 574.

12. K. Bathurst, A. W. Gottfried, D. W. Guerin, P. H. Oliver, and M. C. Ramos. "Family Conflict and Children's Behavior Problems: The Moderating Role of Child Temperament." *Structural Equation Modeling*, 12(2), (2005): 278–98.

13. The National Center for Fathering. "*National Surveys on Fathers and Fathering*," http://www.fathers.com/research/ (accessed June 1, 2005).

14. Ibid.

CHAPTER TWO: HOW WE LOVE TOO MUCH

1. B. Carmichael. *Habits of a Healthy Home: Preparing the Ground in Which Your Children Can Grow* (USA: VMI, 1997).

CHAPTER THREE: WHY WE LOVE TOO MUCH

1. See www.overindulgence.info.

2. See www.mediafamily.org.

3. A. Pietropinto, "Effect of Unhappy Marriages on Children," *Medical Aspects of Human Sexuality* 19, no. 2, (1985): 173–81.

4. H. E. Marano, "Rocking the Cradle of Class," *Psychology Today*, September/October, (2005): 54.

CHAPTER FOUR: WHAT'S THE HARM IN LOVING TOO MUCH?

1. J. I. Clarke and C. Dawson, *Growing Up Again: Parenting Ourselves, Parenting Our Children*, 2nd ed. (Central City, Minnesota: Hazelden, 1998).

2. D. J. Bredehoft and others, "Relationships between childhood overindulgence and family cohesion and adaptability, self-esteem, self-efficacy, self-righteousness, satisfaction with life, dysfunctional attitudes and life distress in late adolescence and young adulthood," http://www.overindulgence.info/Research_Folder/Abstract_Adol_Study.htm (accessed November 28, 2005).

3. B. J. McIntosch, "Spoiled Child Syndrome," *Pediatrics*, 83, no. 1, (1989): 108–15.

4. D. W. Swain, "The Spoiled Child Syndrome," *Changing Family Conference XIV Proceedings*, ed. P. Houston, G. K. Leigh, I. R. Loewen, and D. M. McNulty (Iowa City, IA: The University of Iowa, 1985): 67–71.

5. L. Hausner, *Children of Paradise: Successful Parenting for Prosperous Families* (New York: St. Martin's Press, 1990).

CHAPTER SIX: THE THREE R'S OF HEALTHY LOVE

1. A. Schore, "Affect regulation and the origin of the self: The neurobiology of emotional development" (New York: Lawrence Erlbaum Associates, 1999).

2. Ibid.

CHAPTER SEVEN: LOVING WITHOUT OVERINDULGING

1. D. J. Bredehoft and others, "Perceptions Attributed by Adults to Parental Overindulgence During Childhood," *Journal of Family and Consumer Sciences Education* 16, no. 2, (1998): 1.

CHAPTER EIGHT: LOVING WITHOUT OVERPROTECTING

1. *WordNet*® 2.0, ©2003 Princeton University, http://www.diction-ary.com (accessed December 7, 2005).

2. B. Barber, *Intrusive Parenting: How Psychological Control Affects Children and Adolescents* (Washington, D.C.: American Psychological Association, 2001).

3. M. S. Peck, *The Road Less Traveled: A New Psychology of Love, Traditional Values and Spiritual Growth* (New York: Touchstone, 1980).

4. Well-known quotation of Carl Jung quoted in M. Scott Peck, *The*

Road Less Traveled: A New Psychology of Love, Traditional Values and Spiritual Growth (New York: Touchstone, 1980).

5. J. Ortberg, *If You Want to Walk on Water, You've Got to Get Out of the Boat* (Grand Rapids: Zondervan, 2001).

6. J. I. Clarke and C. Dawson, *Growing Up Again: Parenting Ourselves, Parenting Our Children*, 2nd ed. (Central City, Minnesota: Hazelden, 1998).

7. Eric Erickson, individuation.

8. J. Allen, estimated quotation from performance at the American Association of Christian Counselors World Conference, Nashville, TN, September 2005.

9. B. Simons–Morton and R. Chen, "Latent growth curve analyses of parent influences on drinking progression among early adolescents," *Journal of Studies on Alcohol* 66, no. 1, (2005): 5–13; D. Kieren and B. Munro, "Following the leaders: Parent's influence on adolescent religious activity," *Journal for the Scientific Study of Religion* 26, no. 2, (1987): 7, 249–55.

10. Grace Ketterman, "Godly Parenting," *The Soul Care Bible* (Nashville: Thomas Nelson Publishers, 2001), 826-27.

CHAPTER NINE: LOVING WITHOUT OVERCONTROLLING

1. J. Dobson, *Hide or Seek: How to Build Self-Esteem in Your child* (USA: Baker Books, 1974).

2. Rona Maynard, as cited in baby boomer clues.

3. Adapted from A. Hart, *Stress and Your Child: Know the Signs and Prevent the Harm* (USA: Word, 1992).

4. G. Ketterman, *Parenting the Difficult Child: Commonsense Advice for Identifying and Responding to Your Child's Unique Challenges* (Nashville: Nelson, 1994).

CHAPTER TEN: HOW PARENTS AND KIDS CONNECT

1. J. Bowlby, *Separation: Anxiety and Anger* (USA: The Tavistock Institute of Human Relations, 1973).

2. J. Bowlby, *A Secure Base: Parent-Child Attachment and Healthy Human Development* (New York: Basic Books, 1988).

CHAPTER ELEVEN: BUILDING CLOSENESS WITH YOUR CHILD

1. Bill Carmichael, *Seven Habits of a Healthy Home: Preparing the Ground in Which Your Children Can Grow* (Camp Sherman, OR: VML Publishers, 2002).

2. G. R. Williams, *Quenching the Father Thirst* (The National Center for Fathering, 2003).

3. The National Center for Fathering, *The Extent of Fatherlessness*, http://www.fathers.com/research/extent.html (accessed June 2005).

4. H. Biller, *The Father Factor and the Two-Parent Advantage: Reducing the Paternal Deficit*, presented to the Father-to-Father Working Group Meeting with White House Advisor William Galston, December 17, 1993 and April 15, 1994.

5. B. Hybels and L. Neff, *Too Busy Not to Pray: Slowing Down to Be with God: Including Questions for Reflection and Discussion*, (Downers Grove, IL: InterVarsityPress, 1988).

6. P. F. Kernberg, Saralea E. Chazan, and others, *Children with Conduct Disorders: A Psychotherapy Manual* (USA: Basic Books, 1991).

CHAPTER TWELVE: EMOTION COACHING

1. Daniel Goleman, *Emotional Intelligence* (New York, NY: Bantam, 1995).

2. J. Gottman, J. Declaire, D. Goleman, *Raising an Emotionally Intelligent Child* (New York: Fireside, 1997).

3. Adapted from J. Gottman, L. Katz, C. Hooven, "Parental meta-emotion philosophy and the emotional life of families: Theoretical models and preliminary data," *Journal of Family Psychology* 10, no. 3, (1991): 243–68.

4. L. S. Vygotsky, *Mind in Society: The Development of Higher Psychological Processes* (Cambridge, MA: Harvard University Press, 1978).

5. I. D. Yalom, *Existential Psychotherapy* (New York: Basic Books, 1980).

6. This process has been linked to the development of serious behavior problems in children. It is called the process of coercion; G. Patterson and M. Forgatch, *Parents and Adolescents Living Together, Part 1: The Basics* (Research Press, 2005).

Chapter Thirteen: Effective Discipline for Any Child

1. R. McMahon and R. Forehand, *Helping the Non-Compliant Child,* Second Edition (New York: The Guilford Press, 2003).

2. J. McDowell, "Teens and Lost Values," http://www.apostolic.edu (accessed February, 20 2006).

3. http://www.dictionary.com (accessed December 10, 2005).

4. http://www.dictionary.com (accessed December 10, 2005).

5. J. Dobson, *The New Dare to Discipline* (USA: Tyndale House, 1996).

6. P. D. Meier, D. Ratcliff, F. Rowe, *Christian Child Rearing & Personality Development* (Grand Rapids: Baker Book House, 1977).

7. Ibid.

Chapter Fourteen: Extra-Effort Kids

1. C. U. Tobias, "Bringing Out the Best in a Strong-Willed Child," *The Soul Care Bible*, ed. T. Clinton, (Nelson Bibles, 2001): 830–31.

2. Ibid.

3. American Psychiatric Association, *Diagnostic and Statistical Manual–IV*, Text Revision, 2000.

4. "What Is Attention-Deficit/Hyperactivity Disorder (ADHD)?" September 2005, http://www.cdc.gov/ncbddd/adhd/what.htm (accessed February 20, 2006).

5. "Peer Relationships and ADHD," September 2005, http://www.cdc.gov/ncbddd/adhd/peer.htm (accessed February, 20 2006).